Match Wits with the Harvard MBA's

The $100,000 Inheritance

FAWCETT COLUMBINE   •   NEW YORK

MATCH WITS WITH THE HARVARD MBA's

THE $100,000 INHERITANCE

Tom Fischgrund

Dedicated to my sister, Terry; my brother, Jeff; my niece, Casey; and my son, Ted—Family

Acknowledgments

I would like to thank Jeff Devers and Peter Skolnik for their invaluable advice and help, and Rosalyn Fedro and Donna McIntyre for their typing support.

MATCH WITS
WITH THE
HARVARD
MBA's

THE
$100,000
INHERITANCE

INTRODUCTION

Okay, hot shot. So you'd like to be rich. Who wouldn't? But you figure you're different from the rest of the pack. You're at least as smart as all those people with fancy educations making millions of dollars. You should be making a million dollars too, but instead you're earning only what they use for pocket money. If only you had the chance to show them!

Well here it is—your opportunity to match wits with the best. *Match Wits with the Harvard M.B.A.s* is an exciting investment decision game that lets you square off against the pros—three Harvard Business School grads with combined assets in the millions of dollars. They've paid their academic dues, and it has paid off for them. They know how to make money and make a lot of it. They do it every day.

Now it's your turn to show your investment savvy. How? All you have to do is decide how to invest a $100,000 inheritance and then sit back and watch your money grow. Sound easy? It is. But there's a catch, of course. Just as in real life, not everyone wins in this investment game. You can lose—and lose big. You might even lose a bundle. That's the risk you take when you test yourself against the pros.

But whether you win or lose, you'll enjoy the challenge. And you'll be surprised at how much you learn about how money is really made. If you're a novice, you'll learn all about the fundamentals of investing, from what a CD is to the risks involved in investing in new companies. If you're a more experienced investor, you'll find yourself challenged and entertained as you try to do better than the pros. Whatever your level of expertise, you'll find yourself talking and thinking like an expert.

Are you up to it? Are you ready to accept the challenge of the pros and find out how good you really are? Three experts, all Harvard M.B.A.s, have each played the game. They have made their choices and offered their expert opinion at each decision point. As you make your decisions, you'll want to compare your results with theirs. You think you're good. They *know* they are.

Meet the Experts

They are three Harvard M.B.A.s, class of 1978. Despite their relatively young age, each is very successful at what he or she does. They all work on "the Street" managing and investing hundreds of millions of dollars (other people's money, of course). Their own assets, however, also are quite sizeable and are growing daily. Despite the use of pseudonyms, each of the experts is a real person. A brief profile of each of them follows.

CHATSWORTH "CHAT" MORTON III

Assured, confident, and very astute in money matters, "Chat" has traveled extensively, speaks three languages fluently, and lives life as if there were no yesterdays.

CURRENT POSITION:	Broker to the wealthy (minimum assets $5 million).
ASSETS:	Manhattan Coop, commodities portfolio, venture capital investments, intelligence.
LIABILITIES:	None.
CURRENT SALARY:	$150,000.
S/A RATIO (SALARY TO AGE):	5.
LAST BOOK READ (IF ANY):	*The Bourne Identity*, by Robert Ludlum.
FAVORITE DISH:	Pasta Genovese.
FAVORITE LEISURE TIME PURSUITS:	Foreign films, wine, and exotic things.
FAVORITE INVESTMENT:	Stock index options.
IDOL (FINANCIAL OR OTHER):	Ivan Boesky (Wall Street trader).
INVESTMENT STRATEGY:	Leverage, leverage, leverage (high-risk).
PERSONAL PHILOSOPHY ON MONEY:	"Money is not an end in and of itself, but it sure makes the trip a lot more enjoyable."
QUOTE:	"The best have no conviction. The worst are full of passionate intensity." —Yeats.

JONATHAN WALKER

Reserved by nature but full of energy, the kind of person you would trust large sums of money to—even your own—with a very bright future.

CURRENT POSITION:	Investment banker (large, prestigious New York firm).
ASSETS:	Condominium, Mercedes, real estate (Florida), Treasury bills.
LIABILITIES:	Mortgage, 7% school loans.
CURRENT SALARY:	$160,000 plus bonus.
S/A RATIO (SALARY TO AGE):	6.
LAST BOOK READ (IF ANY):	*Tale of Two Cities* (unabridged version), by Charles Dickens.
FAVORITE DISH:	Prime rib (New York cut).
FAVORITE LEISURE TIME PURSUITS:	A good competitive game of backgammon.
FAVORITE INVESTMENT:	Blue chip corporate bonds.
IDOL (FINANCIAL OR OTHER):	Theodore Roosevelt and Thomas Jefferson.
INVESTMENT STRATEGY:	Long-term capital appreciation (risk-averse).
PERSONAL PHILOSOPHY ON MONEY:	"Money is only a means to acquire more money."
QUOTE:	"Keeping the wheels of finance moving is an awesome responsibility."

GEORGINA GOLD

Outgoing, financially savvy, climbing the financial ladder three rungs at a time, the class of her class.

CURRENT POSITION: First vice president, trading administrator for brokerage firm.

ASSETS: Stocks and bonds, 1967 Ferrari 330 GST, summer home in the Hamptons.

LIABILITIES: Residual loans from business school.

CURRENT SALARY: $170,000.

S/A RATIO (SALARY TO AGE): 7.

LAST BOOK READ (IF ANY): *The Fire Within,* by Carlos Casteneda.

FAVORITE DISH: Sushi.

FAVORITE LEISURE TIME PURSUITS: Racquet ball, skiing, and jogging.

FAVORITE INVESTMENT: Zero coupon municipal bonds that create tax shelters.

IDOL (FINANCIAL OR OTHERWISE): None.

INVESTMENT STRATEGY: Take advantage (opportunistic).

PERSONAL PHILOSOPHY ON MONEY: "Money is a game I enjoy playing."

QUOTE: "There is no reason you can't do everything."

How To Play the Game

Playing the game is easy. Once you've read all about your $100,000 windfall (lucky you!), you'll be presented with investment alternatives—a series of either/or choices that might involve a high-risk investment in a fledgling company, a conservative investment such as a time deposit, or any number of other possibilities such as real estate, futures, bonds, mutual funds, diamonds, gold, and more. Each investment is for a period of one year. All you have to do is pick the alternative you feel will maximize your return—or earn the most money.

But don't worry—you won't be making your decisions in the dark. Before you make each choice, you'll get strategic advice, including a full analysis of the investment, a review of the state of the economy and how it might affect your decision, plus tips from a number of financial sources. Then it's up to you.

Once you've made your choice, it's time to face the consequences—good or bad. You'll be told the results of your decision and the new monetary value of your investment. And you'll see how you stack up against the pros. The three Harvard M.B.A.s will also provide analyses of the decisions you make *(The Experts Speak)* as well as analyses of the decisions they make *(The Experts Strategize).* Some of you will be sadder but wiser; others will be sitting on top of the world. Once you've thought it all over, you'll be ready to try your hand at a new investment choice. At the end of the game, after making your investment decisions, you'll be rated from as high as "Extraordinary" to as low as "Poor." But you don't have to rest on your laurels (or decide you're a hopeless case) the first time around; you can play over and over, since there are sixty-four possible investment paths to choose from.

Investment Strategy

Of course, the most difficult part of the game is making the right choice consistently—and beating the experts. Making money requires skill and luck, and not necessarily in that order. While you can't do much about luck (only successful people seem to have it), you can improve your skills by playing the game in a variety of ways, with several different investment strategies.

While there are a million different possible investment strategies, each tends to follow the old maxim "the greater the return, the higher the risk." In trying to find an appropriate balance between the risk/return trade-off, you should consider what chances you are willing to take in order to become wealthy—or at least less poor.

A high-risk strategy is designed to make a lot of money. The catch is that "high-risk" means that you may also lose a lot of money—just like the high rollers who win and lose millions. High-risk investments tend to favor high-yield options, new high-growth but risky companies, and commodities, among other possibilities.

A risk-averse strategy is another basic way of approaching your investments. Designed to preserve capital, this strategy involves making a moderate amount of money with moderate risk. Investments of this kind tend to be money market funds, municipal bonds, and Treasury bills, among others. Caution and middle class mentality underlie this investment strategy.

An opportunistic strategy falls somewhere between high-risk and risk-averse and means mixing security and growth.

Besides trying these investment strategies, you might want to follow the lead of the three experts, each of whom has chosen one of these investment strategies: high-risk, risk-averse, and opportunistic. See whether they lead you up the road to financial happiness or down the garden path of financial ruin. Maybe you'll make a fortune and maybe you won't.

A final strategy—unfortunately not applicable to real life—

is to take a peek at the end of the book, where the payoffs are tallied. Pick the highest payoff and track it backwards to see how it was achieved. Nothing succeeds like success, after all.

To visualize your choices as you play, you might want to create a decision tree like the one shown, tracking the investment alternatives.

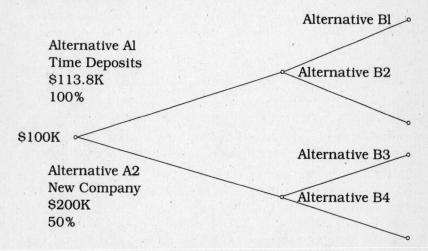

Millions of M.B.A.s and financial analysts swear by the decision tree. Why shouldn't you? Use the decision tree to help you evaluate the alternatives and possible payoffs.

It's time to find out how good you really are. Play the game, and then compare yourself to the Harvard M.B.A.s—if you dare!

THE $100,000 INHERITANCE

Your favorite uncle just died. Bad news. Not really. He left you $100,000, no strings attached. As far as you're concerned it couldn't have come at a better time. You're twenty-five years old. You work for a large insurance company. You make $20,000 a year and have almost no savings, around $150. You are not married. You're comfortable, but by no means living in the lap of luxury.

You have never had a lot of money, but you think big. You decide that this is your big opportunity to be like the rich wheelers and dealers. For the first time you can let your money work for you. But you have to be careful that you don't lose it.

The first thing you do after buying a new car and some new clothes, throwing a small party, and subscribing to *The Wall Street Journal* and *Playboy* or *Playgirl* is to decide where to invest the $100,000. You go to the bank where you have been doing business for the last three years and ask to speak to the bank manager. You wait fifteen minutes while everyone finishes coffee and daily pleasantries. Finally the assistant bank manager, a young fellow who looks and talks as if he received all his clothes and education by mail, asks if he can help you. The bank manager, he explains, is busy working on some important business. You figure they probably looked at your checking and savings account balances (which wouldn't buy a good meal for two at the city's best restaurant) and decided that whatever problem you had could be settled easily. You feel glad that the bank's secretary didn't try to help you.

Your first words to the assistant bank manager are "I just inherited $100,000 and I need some advice on how to invest it. Can you help me?" After you pick up the assistant bank manager from the floor, he quickly shows you into the bank manager's office. She is tall, very proper looking, but a little too conservatively dressed for your taste—pinstripe grey is not your favorite color for any human being, even a bank officer. She is very interested in your circumstances. But alas you realize, like all bankers, she is only interested in your money.

She explains how lucky you are to come to her bank with all its services and expertise. Obviously, she continues, it shows that you either have had money or have the natural wisdom and intelligence to know what to do once you've got it. You think of your bank balances and smile knowingly.

The bank manager then tells you that you have a number of options for investing the $100,000. The first and best option she feels, is to invest in the bank's time deposits in which you'd agree to put your money in an account for a set period of time in exchange for a high interest rate. The current interest rate is 13.8%, which is almost a full 9% higher than the bank's normal 5% savings account rate. Time deposits are very safe, and the rate is guaranteed for the entire period, even if general interest rates decline. Plus, she finishes brightly, you get a free deluxe toaster oven.

While you seem to remember having heard on TV something about substantial penalties for early withdrawal, this option is definitely attractive. At the end of the year your investment will have increased $13,800, and you can always reinvest it should another good opportunity arise.

The bank manager also outlines a number of other alternatives such as stocks, tax-free municipals, and convertible debentures, but each sounds either too confusing or too risky to try at this time. Besides, you want to see which way the economy goes before you try the more esoteric investments. In any case, you need time to think, so you deposit the money in a 5% savings account and tell the bank manager you will get back to her in a week. She thanks you for your time and tells you to call her anytime—even if it's only to talk about your money.

You go home feeling good. After all, you've decided how to

invest your inheritance. That weekend, your neighbor drops by. He's a real smart fellow and basically a nice guy, even if he did go to that well-known Eastern business school in Boston. He works for a new high-tech company called Spreadsheet $ystems, which makes computer software. They are developing financial packages for personal computers—you know, like programs to balance your checkbook and to create financial spreadsheets. Until the inheritance, you barely had enough money to have even a checking account. The only spreadsheets you are familiar with were on your bed. Your friend happens to mention that the company, which was started only two years ago, needs money to expand. While it is currently operating in the red, it is on the verge of coming out with three new programs that will knock the IC (integrated circuit) chips off the competition. The only problem is that the company needs additional capital for marketing and advertising to introduce the new financial programs. Therefore, the company is trying to raise $1 million in blocks of $100,000 each by privately selling common stock to venture capitalists. Your friend explains that venture capitalists are investors who are willing to put money into promising yet risky new companies in exchange for some participation or ownership in the start-up. In this case, each investor will be given 5% of the company's stock for his or her investment. The other 50% will be retained by the founders of the company.

Your friend tells you it's a sure-fire deal—a can't miss, once-in-a-lifetime opportunity. However, he neglects to tell you that it will also pay his salary for the next year. You're not sure whether you trust the guy fully. Most of the time you count your fingers after you shake hands with him. Still, this may be the one-in-a-hundred opportunity you don't want to miss by not even considering it.

Before you decide to invest the inheritance, you want more information on the company. Your friend explains that Spreadsheet $ystems was recently started by two marketing whiz kids who left a competing software manufacturer to strike it rich on their own. Both are considered to be brilliant marketers and well regarded in the field, but, of course, like other brilliant and talented people, they have limited funds available. The company was capitalized on $100,000 begged and borrowed. The first two years were spent setting up the company, stealing computer software designers, and getting ready for the first program introduction. Now that the program is finally ready, the company is down to its last nickel— which is great for a company coming out with a complete home financial planning package.

Your friend may be exuberant, but you'd like to know how much your money will appreciate. While he says he can't guarantee that you'll make any money, he does mention Lotus, a similar company that grew from nothing to sales of millions in only two years. Wouldn't you like to be part of that bonanza?

What should you do? You figure the best place to start is to read the bank's investment advisory newsletter given to you by the over-solicitous bank manager. She said it was free and that you as a valued customer of the bank, would get it monthly. At first you figure it might be worth exactly what you paid for it. But as you start to read, you discover it's really not bad. You also turn on the TV, your other main source of investment information, which is airing a report on the computer software industry.

Bank Investment Advisory Newsletter

The continued growth of consumer prices is still of concern to investors. Prices rose 1.3% last month for an annualized rate of over 14% for the year. This is the sixth month in a row that prices were up over 1%. Financial advisors are questioning how long the recession will last.

Leading economic indicators suggest that recovery may be slow in coming. Only marginal increases were recorded for the last two months. The unemployment rate remains high at over 10%, with little change expected. In addition, there was little real growth in the gross national product (GNP) over the last quarter.

Whatever good news there is remains in a few highly selected industries. Auto and steel sales continue to stagnate.

Interest rates remain high. The prime rate is 16%, while one-month commercial paper is 1.5% lower at 14.5%. Economists predict the high rates and the recession will . . .

THE NOW JONES DIGEST WITH JIM TENKAY

The talk of Silicon Valley these days is computer software companies that supply programs for the personal computer craze. What began only a few short years ago with the introduction of the personal computer has sparked an accompanying software explosion. Some of the new software players are subsidiaries of major companies, such as CBS Software and Random House's Electronic

Publishing Division, while others are start-up ventures such as Spinnaker, Electronic Arts, and Spreadsheet $ystems. The short-term outlook for these companies is very good since computer sales

are booming and the demand for programs is enormous. The key to long-term growth and survival, however, will be the ability to continually produce and market best-selling disks. Today's

success doesn't necessarily guarantee tomorrow's sales, as Visicalc has painfully learned. Only time will tell. However, the outlook for now is rosy.

Investments in this area are recommended.

Established companies with wealthy parents are highly recommended, while newer companies are rated "buy with caution since they entail greater risk." Especially attractive is . . .

DECISION A

A-1 **Do you choose the safe time deposit option,** which will guarantee you 13.8% and leave you free to reinvest? (Turn to page 20.)

or

A-2 **Do you choose the far riskier alternative** of getting in on the ground floor of a growth company in an industry that has made superstars of some while bankrupting others? (Turn to page 25.)

After you have made your decision, see the next two pages for the experts' choices.

THE EXPERTS STRATEGIZE:
A-1. TIME DEPOSITS

Jonathan Walker (Risk-Averse Expert) took this alternative.

I initially took this time deposit option because it offers an incredibly high interest rate, yet is very safe. It is invested in the largest banks in the world. Moreover, it is even insured by the FDIC. How can I lose? We're in a recession. Unemployment is high. If the economy improves, rates may plummet. So I'll make my money now and look for better value later.

Chat Morton (High-Risk Expert) did not take this alternative.

The problem with time deposits at this point is that they just don't generate enough income compared to the high-tech alternative. Since they will not make a lot of money for any length of time, it wouldn't make a great deal of difference in the way I live. With the time deposit I could buy a few more suits and save a little, but now is the time to roll the dice.

Georgina Gold (Opportunistic Expert) took this alternative.

I would take the time deposit alternative. I just received my inheritance. It is too early to tell if success for the computer software company is a sure thing. The industry is still in its infancy. There is plenty of time to wait and watch for developments before investing in today's hula hoop. I am getting a good rate of interest in the time deposits. There always will be an opportunity to invest in the new company down the road (if it's still there).

A-2. NEW COMPUTER SOFTWARE
COMPANY

Chat Morton (High-Risk Expert) took this alternative.

The choice is clear. I would invest in this option. The key things in this industry are to design and to sell new products.

Spreadsheet Systems has those two elements. It was started by two guys who are excellent marketers and who hired excellent program designers. There are no barriers to entry and little money is needed to succeed. One winner buys you a thousand times your money. You are twenty-five years old. What do you have to lose?

Jonathan Walker (Risk-Averse Expert) did not take this alternative.

I don't trust my next-door neighbor. If he's so smart, why does he live next door to me? Who knows how long this start-up will survive? This is the real world, and I would rather not give my money away. Therefore, I would not choose this alternative.

Georgina Gold (Opportunistic Expert) did not take this alternative.

I didn't choose this option because I don't know enough about the industry or the company. Blind dates rarely work, and I view this as a $100,000 blind date. I want to see some development, numbers, and concrete performance over time before I give over my hard-earned inheritance.

(Continued from page 18)

RESULTS:
A-1. TIME DEPOSITS

THE EXPERTS SPEAK
_____ **Jonathan Walker** _____

A very cautious choice, which is okay for someone with new-found money. The economy is not especially healthy; therefore, new companies represent a major risk. Time deposits offer you flexibility. You can earn almost 14% while you see which way the economy goes and what opportunities become available. A very strong holding position, even if it is not necessarily the most profitable one.

You decided to play it safe. After all, you're new at the game. You don't have a lot of money in the bank, and for one year you wanted security. But security has a price. You made almost $14,000. Big deal. At that rate you are never going to get rich. You realize you don't have enough money to invest to live off the income, unless you move to an abandoned building and eat canned cat food. Not you. You're a Dom Pérignon and caviar person. The problem is where to invest.

A person with money is never without friends. The bank officer calls you regularly, especially now that your time deposits have almost matured. She inquires about your health, happiness—and especially your wealth.

Your friend from the software company also stops by. In his quiet, unassuming Eastern business school manner, he tells you that you blew it. The first of the three financial programs came out and was a smashing success. As a result, the original offering of Spreadsheet Systems, which sold out, has doubled in value. Having snatched defeat from the jaws of victory, you ask your friend what he now would recommend. Never one to shirk from giving free advice on anything (the less he knows about a subject, the more he has to say), your friend says that you should be adventuresome. You could either invest in new technologies such as computer software or in growth areas such as real estate. Since you missed the boat on the former, why not try owning property? He just happens to know an apartment building going coop that you can get in on at the insider's or reduce price. Once the building actually goes coop, you can in turn flip or sell your coop apartment at a large profit, maybe even double or triple your original investment—especially since the entire building is being renovated. No one since the Indians, who sold Manhattan for $24, ever lost money on real estate. You have visions of being landed gentry, even if your estate is only 1,200 square feet with two bedrooms. What could go wrong?

At this point, the bank officer calls. She's concerned. You haven't renewed your time deposits yet. Is everything all right? When you explain that you feel the time deposits are too conservative, she suggests a more adventurous option: foreign bank money market special reserve funds, which buy

CDs from Central American and Eastern European banks. While they still are safe, they yield 14.9% annually. Sure, you can make more money elsewhere, she tells you, but you can lose money elsewhere too. When you tell her of the real estate opportunity your friend brought to your attention, she says that's great. But what if the apartment doesn't go coop; what if you can't resell it; what if interest rates don't fall; and what if the building isn't renovated right away?

You reply that your friend predicts a 100% to 200% increase. She responds that only hot air and taxes continually rise without fail. With the money market funds you're almost guaranteed a decent return.

Again before you make your decision, you pick up the bank's monthly investment advisory newsletter. You also review some information on the proposed coop apartment given to you by your friend.

Bank Investment Advisory Newsletter

The economy is starting to pick up. For the past two months, the consumer price index (CPI) has gained only .8% per month, which could bring the annual rate to less than 10%. A major cause of this drop is the lowering of interest rates. Spurred on by a reduction in the T-bill rate, banks have lowered their prime rate to 13% from a high of 16% only six months ago.

Consumer purchases also have begun to rebound. The major car makers reported increased sales of 16% over a year ago and 10% over last month. Housing starts, long stagnant, increased 3% for the past three months. New orders for durable goods and capital investment also are up.

Interest rates are expected to continue to fall. The only bleak spot on the economic picture is unemployment, which remains in double-digit figures. Still, as the economy improves . . .

Apartment coop Checklist
  Insider's price $115,000
  outsider's price $150,000

Pluses
- Conversion to take place within a year.
- Market value of comparable selling units is over $200,000.
- Location and schools are excellent.
- Building to be completely renovated within one year, which should further enhance value.

Minuses
- Building doesn't go coop.
- Apartment right above aromatic Indian restaurant.
- Insects of unknown origin.

DECISION B

The current value of your investment is $113,800. Tough luck, your investment is 20% below the average of the experts.

B-1 **Do you become a real estate mogul and buy an apartment coop** at the insider's price, hoping to resell it for a substantial gain? (Turn to page 30.)

or

B-2 **Do you invest in the special reserve funds,** which will increase your investment by $16,956? (Turn to page 34.)

After you have made your decision, turn to the next page for the experts' choices.

THE EXPERTS STRATEGIZE:
B-1. APARTMENT COOP

Georgina Gold (Opportunistic Expert) took this alternative.

I took the coop investment because I always try to buy value. The market estimate of the value is $200K. I am paying only $115K. Even with a softening in the marketplace of 25%, I could still easily get a return of 30% from my money, which I'll take anytime. When opportunity knocks on the real estate door, answer it.

Jonathan Walker (Risk-Averse Expert) did not take this alternative.

I don't invest in areas I don't know a lot about or where there is a risk I can lose my money (i.e., if the apartment doesn't go coop, I will have paid $115K to rent an apartment). You can make a lot of money from real estate if you're very knowledgeable or very lucky. With money market funds you don't need knowledge or luck. Therefore, I chose the safe 14.9% alternative. I'm always safe and never sorry.

B-2. SPECIAL RESERVE FUNDS

Jonathan Walker (Risk-Averse Expert) took this alternative.

I took the money funds option. I already am beginning to see the effects of compounding. At this rate, I'll double my money in five years. Interest rates are going my way. While I haven't been struck by financial lightning, I am not in pain either. My assets are growing, and I am still happy with my life-style.

Georgina Gold (Opportunistic Expert) did not take this alternative.

In order to be a good investor, you have to be able to judge relative risk and return. The return offered by the real estate alternative far outweighs the additional risk you incur relative to the money market fund. There is great upside potential in real estate. Furthermore, I like the idea of owning property. It is tangible wealth.

(Continued from page 18)

RESULTS:
A-2. NEW COMPUTER SOFTWARE COMPANY

THE EXPERTS SPEAK
Chat Morton

You picked a risky alternative and fortunately did well. Most new companies fail, especially in hard economic times. On the other hand, the 5% share you bought for $100,000 gave you a reasonable percentage of the company. Unless by nature you are a gambler, in the future you might exercise a little more caution.

You did it. You played the long shot and won. The first program from Spreadsheet $ystems was a blockbuster success, selling over 75,000 copies. *Computer Age* magazine called it "the greatest program ever made." Great sales are predicted far into the future—or for at least six months, whichever comes first. Based on this initial success, the well-known investment analysts with the brokerage house of Casey and Beth call the future of the company exciting. In fact, venture capitalists have even offered to buy you out for twice what you paid, or $200,000.

But alas, the road to fortune and fame is not often smooth. The company needs money to exploit its initial success. To introduce the two new financial programs, the company estimates it needs an additional $3 million for marketing, advertising, and product development. A decision is made to issue additional shares. While you realize that it would be difficult for the company to succeed without the additional funding, you're also aware that more shares will lessen your percentage of the profit.

The real issue, however, is whether you believe that the company will have three successful financial programs in a row. Or whether, given the volatility of the industry and the public, you should take the money and run. You could always invest it in foreign bank money market special reserve funds at 14.9%, after all. On the other hand, with a growing economy the company might just succeed—in spite of the increasing competition in the software industry. Your friend from the company talks of another 100% increase. While you doubt that figure, you secretly think even 50% wouldn't be bad. Of course, high risk doesn't always guarantee high return. Some people actually lose money investing in a new company with a limited track record.

Again, before you make your decision, you pick up the bank's monthly investment advisory newsletter. You also glance over some financial and sales information on the computer software company given to you by your friend.

Bank Investment Advisory Newsletter

The economy is starting to pick up. For the past two months, the consumer price index (CPI) has gained only .8% per month, which could bring the annual rate to less than 10%. A major cause of this drop is the lowering of interest rates. Spurred on by a reduction in the T-bill rate, banks have lowered their prime rate to 13% from a high of 16% only six months ago.

Consumer purchases also have begun to rebound. The major car makers reported increased sales of 16% over a year ago and 10% over last month. Housing starts, long stagnant, increased 3% for the past three months. New orders for durable goods and capital investments also are up.

Interest rates are expected to continue to fall. The only bleak spot on the economic picture is unemployment, which remains in double-digit figures. Still, as the economy improves . . .

SPREADSHEET $YSTEMS
CHAIRMAN'S MESSAGE TO SHAREHOLDERS

Initial sales of the first financial software package were double the original estimate of 37,000. At $60@ wholesale, sales generated revenues of $4.5M. The cost of producing the disks was $1.5M ($20@), leaving a gross income of $3M.

Note that $1.5M was spent on advertising and marketing with $250,000 expended primarily on R&D. This leaves a profit or net income of $1.25M. The profit was reinvested in the company to expand production facilities, which are currently operating on double shifts, and to provide continued advertising support for current and planned software introductions. Future advertising expenditures need to be even greater to remain competitive in an increasingly crowded field. Additional monies will be used to continue to develop new products.

Management is lean with a central staff of only eight, including the two principals. The company continues to spend heavily on R&D so that it can develop new programs. Three new engineers/designers were hired to replace the four who resigned.

Based on the initial sales, Spreadsheet $ystems is optimistic . . .

DECISION B

The current value of your investment is $200,000. Congratulations, your investment is 40% above the average of the experts.

B-3 *Do you continue to keep your money in the goose-that-laid-the-golden computer software?* (Turn to page 38.)

or

B-4 *Do you sell your participation and switch your money to a more conservative foreign bank money market alternative,* paying a more-than-respectable 14.9%, or $29,800? (Turn to page 43.)

After you make your decision, see the next page for the experts' choices.

THE EXPERTS STRATEGIZE: B-3. SPREADSHEET $YSTEMS

Chat Morton (High-Risk Expert) took this alternative.

I would definitely stick with Spreadsheet $ystems. The economy is improving. Disposable income is up, as are consumer purchases. Spreadsheet $ystems is hot, which indicates it is doing something right. Success breeds success. Profits are being reinvested in the company. Moreover, the company still is relatively lean and mean despite the growth of administrative expenses. The only bad news is that four engineers resigned, but they were replaced. Overall, the industry is strong and there is still a lot of room for growth. All of which means I can make a lot of money with this company.

B-4. MONEY MARKET FUND

Chat Morton (High-Risk Expert) did not take this alternative.

I did not choose the money market alternative because Spreadsheet $ystems is right where you want it to be. The company has had one success already and has new products ready to go. The numbers, sales, net income, etc., look good, so why change horses now? Besides, there isn't enough income in money market funds to make me stop dreaming about my Jaguar.

(Continued from page 23)

RESULTS:
B-1. APARTMENT COOP

THE EXPERTS SPEAK
Georgina Gold

Real estate is a prime example of the law of supply and demand. When demand outstrips supply and you can't easily expand the supply, the value goes up. That is the lesson of real estate. In addition, if you really do pay under market price (i.e., the insider's price), then you have bought additional value. Why work if you can get rich owning real estate?

Nothing went right and you still made a great deal of money. That's real estate. It took longer than expected for the apartment to go coop. Instead of two months, it took six months for the paperwork to be completed. The renovation also is taking longer. What originally was envisioned as a one-year plan has now been stretched to five. You only hope your children see a renovated apartment building. Finally, interest rates fell, but only by one-half percent. Mortgage money is still very expensive. Despite these problems, your investment increased just less than 59% to $181,600, which is very respectable, but nothing like the 100% to 200% return you had hoped for. In addition, the likelihood of making a lot more money on the coop is limited until the renovation is complete. It's obviously time to sell. But what to do next is the question.

Your friend from the computer software company says you're in luck. He needs money badly to pay off debts on some investments that soured and is willing to sell you his shares (2.85%) in Spreadsheet Systems for $181,600. How ironic. That's exactly what your coop apartment is worth. But you wonder whether you're trading one problem child for another. Don't worry, he counsels, the company has had three successful software programs and is now thinking of going public. If that happens, your $181,600 could be worth millions. Who knows how high the public will bid up the price of the company?

If this is such a great deal, why is your friend selling, you wonder. Reading your mind and seeing you hesitate, your friend responds (in his most honest voice possible) that some debts—like time—wait for no man or woman. You question no further.

You think of the alternatives. Your bank officer recommends safe short-term corporate bonds paying slightly more than 11%. These bonds are debt obligations of corporations and are used to raise money for a short period of time. No risk, and all you have to do is watch your money grow. But then again, her tastes are not expensive. She shops at K Mart for clothes. You'd like to be more adventuresome and make more money in the new company. But what if the public offering is a flop? Then you'll be a flop too.

Again, you review the monthly economic forecast and the latest progress report from Spreadsheet Systems.

Bank Investment Advisory Newsletter

Interest rates continue to fall. The top three American banks announced last week that they were lowering their prime rate another 1/2% to 12%. Even lower rates are forecast amidst speculation that the Federal Reserve Board will be lowering the discount rate (the rate the federal government charges banks) in the near future.

The recovery continues to pick up, with large sales gains reported in auto, communications, and housing. However, the recovery is still not universal, as some industries such as steel seem immune to better times. Even within historically profitable sectors some companies are having a difficult time becoming profitable again.

On the whole, the economic mood of business leaders is positive. A rash of new issues coming to market are being bought at a brisk pace by investors.

SPREADSHEET $YSTEMS
CHAIRMAN'S MESSAGE TO SHAREHOLDERS

Sales continue to boom. The two new financial programs had sales of 62,500 and 32,500 respectively, with Spreadsheet's first financial software package remaining strong with sales of 25,000 for the period. Revenues were $7,200,000 for the second year of operation.

Manufacturing costs of $2,760,000 rose slightly (15%) to handle the increased volume. Marketing costs of $2,250,000 were also up (50%) because of an increasingly competitive marketplace for computer software. Despite this, R&D expenditures at $360,000 remained constant at 5% of sales, while administrative costs of $330,000 increased from less than 1% of sales to almost 5%. Net income for the period was $1,500,000. The company distributed its first dividend of $500,000 to the original participants.

Despite a six-month delay, new programs on the computer boards look promising, with new introductions planned for later in the year (details to follow). The company feels the strength of its first programs provides a good springboard for . . .

DECISION C

The current value of your investment is *$181,600*. Tough luck, your investment is 67% below the average of the experts.

C-1 **Do you play conservatively and invest in short-term corporate bonds** yielding just above 11%, or $20,004? (Turn to page 47.)

or

C-2 **Do you buy your friend's shares in Spreadsheet Systems** in anticipation of the company's going public—and of the public's going wild over the new wunderkind venture? (Turn to page 53.)

After you have made your decision, turn to the next page for the experts' choices.

THE EXPERTS STRATEGIZE: C-1. SHORT-TERM CORPORATE BONDS

Georgina Gold (Opportunistic Expert) did not take this alternative.

The 11% yield being offered by corporate bonds is not enough to whet my investment appetite. I realize that the bonds are very safe, but I want my dollars to work as hard as I do. This investment is only working six hours a day, like most financial advisors and brokers. The other alternative, Spreadsheet $ystems, at least has some potential of increasing my wealth.

C-2. SPREADSHEET $YSTEMS

Georgina Gold (Opportunistic Expert) took this alternative.

Once again, the key to good investing is identifying value. My friend who has the company stock for sale needs money and therefore is willing to sell the stock relatively cheaply. The company looks very good. It is well run with a good track record to date. The economy is improving, and the investing public is hungry for new issues. Rich people get richer because they have the money and the patience to buy opportunity. This is an opportunity too good to pass up.

(Continued from page 23)

RESULTS: B-2. SPECIAL RESERVE FUNDS

THE EXPERTS SPEAK
—————————— Georgina Gold ——————————

Good grief, you're conservative! You continue to pick conservative alternatives. However, since interest rates are at near-

record levels, you can't go too far wrong. It is difficult to believe that interest rates will remain that high. Therefore, you
might want to start looking at more aggressive opportunities,

---

No one could fault you for going the safe route. After all, you
made almost 15% on your investment. However, no one will
praise you either. Had you invested in the real estate, your
money would have increased at least 59%. You're pleased with
what you did, but not really satisfied. You need to make more
money. Maybe you should be more aggressive.

Imbued with the desire to make more money faster, you
visit your banker. You tell her that 15% may be okay for reti-
rees and conservative bankers, but it's not all right with you.
You want a better yield; you're ready to play hardball.

Your banker responds that anything's possible, but you
should always remember that the greater the potential return, the higher the risk. But if a high return is what you
want, then she knows just the broker for you—her husband,
Nathaniel. She calls him up, and he meets you in only ten
minutes. Money has a way of speeding up the often slow and
cumbersome wheels of finance. Her husband seems like a
nice guy, even if he is a salesman. Besides, you can use the
free pen and calendar he gave you as you shook his hand
when he introduced himself.

Nathaniel states that if you want to earn a greater return,
he knows just what you need—options. Options, he explains,
are an institutional guessing game in which you try to predict
whether the price of stocks or other investments will go up or
down within a certain period of time. For example, for $1 per
share you buy the right for one year to purchase a stock at
$100 per share. It currently sells for $90. If the stock goes up
to $102, you make $2 less the $1 you invested, for a $1 profit,
or 100% return. If after a year the value stays below $100,
you let your option lapse. Nathaniel explains that the spread
between the call, or selling price, and the market value is the
stuff millionaires are made of. You think option certificates
are also the stuff bathrooms are wallpapered with. In any
case, if you want to make money, you have to take some risks.

Nathaniel recommends options issued by a top performer, American Diversified Industries. The company is blue-chip all the way. In the past five years, American Diversified Industries sales have doubled and its profits have increased three-fold. As a result, the stock price has grown an average of 15% per year. Therefore, you can make a lot of money. It sounds too good to be true. That worries you.

When Nathaniel sees you hesitate he suggests you put half your money in the blue-chip options, which he predicts will return 20%, and the other half in safe, although low-yielding, time deposits. On the other hand, you could continue to put all your principal into time deposits, although at the now-lower rate of 11%. What's an investor to do?

Again you review the economic newsletter from the bank. You also pick up a magazine article on American Diversified Industries, as you look for those crystal ball indicators which you hope will shed light on the future.

Bank Investment Advisory Newsletter

Interest rates continue to fall. The top three American banks announced last week that they were lowering their prime rate another 1/2% to 12%. Even lower rates are forecast amidst speculation that the Federal Reserve Board will be lowering the discount rate (the rate the federal government charges banks) in the near future.

The recovery continues to pick up, with large sales gains reported in auto, communications, and housing. However, the recovery is still not universal, as some industries such as steel seem immune to better times. Even within historically profitable sectors some companies are having a difficult time becoming profitable again.

On the whole, the economic mood of business leaders is positive. A rash of new issues coming to market are being bought at a brisk pace by investors.

Street Scene Magazine

"STILL GOING STRONG"

American Diversified Industries continues to experience unprecedented growth. Each of its highly diversified operations—fast food, fashion, financial services, and phone equipment—is growing at an average rate of 50%. Moreover, the potential for growth is explosive, since all these categories are rapidly expanding. The company is closely monitoring all of its diversified companies and is continually looking for new opportunities and acquisitions.

Sales are now $500 million and are expected to climb to over $600 million by the end of the year. With American Diversified Industries' constant scrutiny and cost control, profit margins likewise should grow 20%. Wall Street analysts are expecting even higher sales and profits. The company will do its best to meet these expectations . . .

DECISION C

The current value of your investment is *$130,756*. Tough luck, your investment is 33% below the average of the experts.

C-3 *Do you put half your money in options and the other half in time deposits*, hoping the risk will pay off handsomely? (Turn to page 56.)

or

C-4 *Do you invest all your money in conservative 11% time deposits* that pay $14,383 and then look for risk and excitement on television? (Turn to page 61.)

After you have made your decision, turn to the next page for the experts' choices.

THE EXPERTS STRATEGIZE:
C-3. OPTIONS/TIME DEPOSITS

Jonathan Walker (Risk-Averse Expert) did not take this alternative.

Most options players are losers, since options are a very risky investment. Nobody is giving away anything for free here. I don't want to be a millionaire; I want to have my money and to make it grow over time. When options expire, so does my money. I don't want to see my money die.

C-4. TIME DEPOSITS

Jonathan Walker (Risk-Averse Expert) took this alternative.

Certainly 11% is a very attractive rate. I have no risk. I can relax and count my money as it grows and basically look for safe alternatives when these time deposits need to be reinvested. I am still making 70% of my salary for doing nothing here. That's not a small amount of money to me, and I prefer to keep it safe.

(Continued from page 28)

RESULTS:
B-3. SPREADSHEET SYSTEMS

THE EXPERTS SPEAK
Chat Morton

Good. Stick with the winners and you'll rarely go wrong. Just be sure you can separate the winners from the losers. Spreadsheet Systems has started to build up a good track record, which is what most professionals look for in new businesses. The company also seems to be able to develop software the computer public wants. Another good sign for a new consumer products company is that the economy is expanding, with advances in consumer purchases.

Take heed, however, that this success has some legs in an industry where public whims and desires change very rapidly.

Are you really that brilliant or just a good guesser? The next two financial programs also were highly successful. They quickly climbed to the top of the computer software charts and seem destined to become standards in the field. But the first program, while continuing to do well, is beginning to show signs of weakness after six months as a sales leader. So much for permanence.

Your financial condition is very healthy. The success of the two new programs has increased your holdings by an estimated 20%. Your total growth in only two years has been a whopping 140%. Not bad for an amateur.

That's not the only good news. There are rumblings in the stock market that the company is going public. That would be a great opportunity for you, because if you could sell your shares on the open market, your paper profit would turn into liquid assets. You can hardly wait. A month before the anticipated date of the public offering, your friend calls you and tells you the company is interested in repurchasing your shares. They are willing to pay you a hefty $319,200 cash, a 33% premium. You could put the cash into one of those new asset management accounts the banker told you about and get a low but guaranteed 10%. The advantage of an asset management account, explains your banker, is that you generally get a higher interest rate by centralizing all your accounts (checking, savings, stocks, etc.) into one, while still keeping your money highly liquid. Thus, you could always reinvest at a moment's notice should the right opportunity come along.

On the other hand, you figure the founders would never have offered you big bucks if the company was not going public. Maybe you should hold out for more money. You call your friend to find out whether the offering price is negotiable. He tells you no. In fact, the offer is good for one week. Do you take a sure $319 grand or wait for the public to make you a millionaire?

With a growing economy you feel the time is right for a public offering, especially since the company has had three hits in a row. What could go wrong? The computer software industry is booming. In fact, five new companies are entering the field, some with big money behind them. Sales of disks are up 300% over last year. Except for a few naysayers who continually warn of a shakeout in an already crowded field, everything is coming up electrodes, chips, and CRTs.

Again you review the monthly economic forecast and the latest progress report from Spreadsheet Systems.

Bank Investment Advisory Newsletter

Interest rates continue to fall. The top three American banks announced last week that they were lowering their prime rate another 1/2% to 12%. Even lower rates are forecast amidst speculation that the Federal Reserve Board will be lowering the discount rate (the rate the federal government charges banks) in the near future.

The recovery continues to pick up, with large sales gains reported in auto, communications, and housing. However, the recovery is still not universal, as some industries such as steel seem immune to better times. Even within historically profitable sectors some companies are having a difficult time becoming profitable again.

On the whole, the economic mood of business leaders is positive. A rash of new issues are being bought at a brisk pace by investors.

SPREADSHEET $YSTEMS
CHAIRMAN'S MESSAGE TO SHAREHOLDERS

Sales continue to boom. The two new financial programs had sales of 62,500 and 32,500 respectively, with

Spreadsheet's first financial software package remaining strong with sales of 25,000 for the period. Revenues were $7,200,000 for the second year of operation.

Manufacturing costs of $2,760,000 rose slightly (15%) to handle the increased volume. Marketing costs of $2,250,000 were also up (50%) because of an increasingly competitive marketplace for computer software. Despite this, R&D expenditures at $360,000 remained constant at 5% of sales, while administrative costs of $330,000 increased from less than 1% of sales to almost 5%. Net income for the period was $1,500,000. The company distributed its first dividend of $500,000 to the original participants.

Despite a six-month delay, new programs on the computer boards look promising, with new introductions planned for later in the year (details to follow). The company feels the strength of its first programs provides a good springboard for . . .

DECISION C

The current value of your investment is *$240,000*. Congratulations, your investment is 63% above the average of the experts.

C-5 *Do you accept the founders' offer of $319,200,* count your blessings (and cash), *and then squirrel away your money in a new 10% asset management account?* (Turn to page 66.)

or

C-6 *Is now the right moment for the market to value your shares* and make you a prince (or a pauper)? (Turn to page 70.)

After you have made your decision, turn to the next page for the experts' choices.

THE EXPERTS STRATEGIZE:
C-5. SPREADSHEET $YSTEMS SELL-OFF/ASSET MANAGEMENT ACCOUNT

Chat Morton (High-Risk Expert) did not take this alternative.

Although I am finally turning my back on what is substantial income, I feel the company is on the verge of going big time. There are risks in turning down the sure thing, such as indications that competition is becoming cutthroat (as marketing costs rise), the fact that the company distributed dividends too early in its development, and the lack of new program announcements. On the other hand, while all I have to lose is my initial investment, the upside is near and could be in the millions of dollars.

C-6. SPREADSHEET $YSTEMS

Chat Morton (High-Risk Expert) took this alternative.

There is no question this is the right choice. The founders are willing to pay me over three times what I put in. Why do they want me out? I took all the risks in the beginning. Now I want a share of the glory. Greed is in the air. The market is strong. The bulls who have been corralled for years are now running wild—and I have what they want. The company is rolling and reinvesting. The only real bad news is that margins have not expanded, but that is not unusual, particularly in high-growth companies. Spreadsheet $ystems is a winner.

(Continued from page 28)

RESULTS:
B-4. MONEY MARKET FUND

THE EXPERTS SPEAK
Chat Morton

It's obvious your knowledge of good computer software and consumer needs is as good as your investment knowledge. Both stink. Spreadsheet $ystems was going strong. Why change investments in midstream? It only hurts your cash flow. Be careful when you change strategies. It may be harmful to your financial health.

Safety first. You felt there was no sense in pressing your luck based on whether or not a few computerphiles felt your program was good. You chose to profit from your initial risk taking and picked a relatively safe 14.9% return from a money market fund. Unfortunately, you guessed wrong. The public seeks financial aid wherever it can get it.

The next two financial programs turned out to be highly successful. More important, they have fueled the rumors that the company will go public, which would have greatly expanded your potential profit. Oh well, there's always the lottery to make money.

The picture is not all bleak, however. After all, in only one year's time you have more than doubled your money. Not bad. The question now is, what do you do next?

You feel bankers are too conservative. Stock brokers are too salesmen-oriented. What you feel you need is a money manager or financial advisor. You remember that your cousin Leonard works for some kind of financial services company. Leonard was always the black sheep of the family, although not because he wasn't successful—on the contrary, he was immensely rich. But he wouldn't share it. Who said everything is relative? However, now that you have money he might deign to talk to you as if you were almost his equal.

You call him up and ask for advice. He's happy to hear from you. In fact, because you're family, he'll even cut his management fee in half. He suggests a number of alternatives.

On the more conservative side you could try a short-term bond fund, which is a diversified fund of bonds or corporate debt with a maturity of one year or less (but which can be sold at any time). In fact, Leonard's company has a fund paying 14% (which is way above most current time deposits), almost 2% above what most other funds are now paying. It's a bit risky, but that's why it's paying more interest.

If you really want to be bold, you could invest in commodity futures. What you do is agree to buy X thousand bushels of wheat at a certain price within the next year. If the price of wheat goes up, you sell your futures and make money. If it goes down, you take a beating. You wonder, since you're a novice at investing, whether commodity futures trading makes sense for you at this time. It seems to go against your grain, so to speak. But Leonard says that since there is always a drought somewhere, food is a valuable resource, and you could double your money quickly. You look out your window and notice that it's started to rain.

Investing in grain futures is like taking the New York subway at 5 P.M. during rush hour: a lot of people do it, but it is not for the timid or weak of heart. You are just as likely to lose your money as to make it.

Again you review the economic newsletter from the bank and a monthly pamphlet on commodities called "Staple Items."

Bank Investment Advisory Newsletter

Interest rates continue to fall. The top three American banks announced last week that they were lowering their prime rate another 1/2% to 12%. Even lower rates are forecast amidst speculation that the Federal Reserve Board will be lowering the discount rate (the rate the federal government charges banks) in the near future.

The recovery continues to pick up, with large sales gains reported in auto, communications, and housing. However, the recovery is still not universal, as some industries such as steel seem immune to better times. Even within historically profitable sectors some companies are having a difficult time becoming profitable again.

▤STAPLE ITEMS▤
A REPORT ON COMMODITIES

Supplies of grain crops remained large due to high starting inventories and a bumper crop. This has put a damper on wheat futures. Moreover, good weather is expected to swell inventories further. The USDA has announced it will not do additional buying this year. There are rumors that the U.S. is negotiating with the Soviet Union on some large grain sales. If this is true, such a sale would draw down the inventory, which would tighten supply and boost prices, turning the entire market around. Washington continues to deny a deal is imminent, although it has confirmed that talks are being held.

DECISION C

The current value of your investment is $229,800.* Con-gratulations, your investment is 18% above the average of the experts.

C-7 **Do you invest in Leonard's** relatively safe but profitable **14% short-term bond fund?** (Turn to page 74.)

or

C-8 **Do you shoot the works on grain futures** and hope to reap the benefits? (Turn to page 78.)

After you have made your decision, see the next page for the experts' comments.

THE EXPERTS STRATEGIZE:
C-7. SHORT-TERM BOND FUND

Jonathan Walker (Risk-Averse Expert)—Commentary

This is an exceptionally high-returning fund. With the prime at 12% and declining, the ability to earn 14% guaranteed is a tremendous opportunity. The bond funds are invested in debt issues of major corporations in the United States. Notwithstanding a depression, this return is very safe and very high.

C-8. GRAIN FUTURES

Georgina Gold (Opportunistic Expert)—Commentary

The commodity market is extremely active with speculators and hedgers participating from around the world. The good and the bad news about futures is leverage, i.e., a small amount of money can control a sizeable future commitment. However, eight out of ten people who play futures lose, which makes the other two people extremely happy. Futures are a zero-sum game. For each winner, there is a loser. Therefore, the question for an individual speculator is, how lucky do you feel?

(Continued from page 33)

RESULTS:
C-1. SHORT-TERM CORPORATE BONDS

THE EXPERTS SPEAK
Chat Morton

Stupid move. When you have a chance to capitalize on a hot company going public, take it. Valuation of a new company is generally tied to the earnings of a company, i.e., the public pays a certain multiple times earnings. Since earnings were

$1.5 million and it is not uncommon for the public to pay 10X, 15X, or even 20X earnings, it was foolish not to take the risk. Your share of the company (almost 3%) was worth a lot more than the 11% you made.

An 11% return is what you can expect if you get all your investment advice from a banker or government publications. Horrible, when you consider the alternative. Spreadsheet $ystems did go public and the market reception was only lukewarm. The public's concern about an overcrowded field and a possible shakeout caused them to pay a very low P/E, or price-earnings ratio. The P/E ratio, as you know, is often used by investors to evaluate the fairness or relative value of the price of a stock. This meant that instead of making 20X earnings (which is a high multiple) on Spreadsheet $ystems, you would have made only 7X earnings. However, translated into dollars and cents, 7X earnings of $1.5 million is $10.5 million, of which your share (almost 3%) would have been worth $299,250, or nearly $100,000 more than you made.

You conquered your greed and it cost you dearly. Now, more than ever, you want to make a killing. Some people never learn. You call up your banker, although you realize a banker is the last person who knows how to make real money. You ask for a recommendation. She suggests her husband, Nathaniel the broker. You only hope he doesn't make you that way—broker. But you'll try anything—once.

Nathaniel looks at you and your situation and says that the bonds that you invested in really aren't that bad. The problem is that there is no upside potential, even if the company takes off. Therefore, he advises convertible debentures—that is, debt (like bonds) which can be converted into stock for a set number of shares. They pay less interest (only 7%) but offer significant opportunity. He suggests convertible bonds of one of the Fortune 100, American Electric. These bonds are rated AA, which is the highest rating a bond can receive. Moreover, they are convertible at a profit if the stock grows more than 20%.

The other alternative Nathaniel recommends is equity mutual funds currently yielding 12%, a rate that could go higher (or lower) depending on the market. An equity mutual fund, he explains, is a fund composed of stocks or equities as opposed to bond mutual funds, commodity mutual funds, and so forth. The mutual fund he suggests, the Atlas Zenith Fund, invests only in star performers of the Fortune 500. It has grown an average of 16% per year, although it has varied from 4% to 30% over the last five years. Still, it is one of the premier mutual funds for both growth and security.

You review the financial and economic data you have, grab a bite to eat, watch TV, and then make a decision.

Bank Investment Advisory Newsletter

Recovery from the recession stutters. After a year in which interest and inflation rates steadily declined, both measures of economic vitality took a turn for the worse. Aggravated by a more restrictive money supply, the discount rate increased a full percent. The prime rate rose a point to 13%. Capital spending on plant and equipment likewise has suffered. Consumer spending is expected to decline unless interest rates can be lowered. The real key is inflation. If inflation remains stable at 10% or declines, actions of the Fed are likely to be eased.

Despite high rates, certain segments of the economy held their own. Car sales increased 10% over a year ago. With more people traveling, airlines showed a whopping 20% gain. However, banks and electric utilities remain anemic.

The GNP grew at a slow 2.3% pace. Government spending continues to trouble economists. Leading economic analysts question whether the ever-growing federal deficit can be controlled. Unemployment also remains bleak at 10%. The major question now is whether this halt in the recovery is temporary or whether the three plagues of the recession—high interest rates, high inflation, and high unemployment—have returned to stay.

Street Scene Magazine

"A HIGHLY CHARGED COMPANY"

American Electric (AE) continues to be the stellar performer in its category. It has introduced a series of new products: longer-lasting light bulbs, new digital/analog switches, and motors, all of which are highly rated. The company has picked its markets carefully, choosing only those with growth rates above 20%. Finally, the company has achieved even stronger profit margins through a combination of phasing out old plants and innovating new techniques. Sales and profits grew at a very healthy 25% last year.

American Electric has largely financed its rapid expansion through ongoing operations and new stock issues. Faced with continued future growth, American Electric is floating a $100 million convertible debenture issue. The bonds are rated as attractive given the stock's spectacular performance in the past— 20% growth per year for the last three years. Strongly recommended by the major brokerage houses, American Electric . . . .

DECISION D

The current value of your investment is *$201,604*. Tough luck, your investment is 38% below the average of the experts.

D-1 *Do you purchase convertible debentures* with a 7% rate but great upside potential if the stock price soars? (Turn to page 83.)

or

D-2 *Do you pick a safer equity mutual fund* with a 12% rate (more or less)? (Turn to page 86.)

After you have made your decision, turn to the next page for the experts' comments.

THE EXPERTS STRATEGIZE:
D-1. CONVERTIBLE DEBENTURES

Georgina Gold (Opportunistic Expert)—Commentary

There are two ways to make money with convertible bonds. First, if general interest rates decline, the bond value goes up. This is because the bond's interest rate is fixed, which means you can earn greater interest from the bond than from an obligation issued at the current, and lower, market rate. The bond value is then adjusted upward to make the bond value equivalent to new lower yielding bond issues. Second, if the stock price rises, so does the value of the debenture. Both seem possible in this case. Despite a temporary setback, interest rates should begin to decline again from the present high levels. You can't find a better company than American Electric. It has had an excellent record. The company's profits have been growing.

The bonds are rated as attractive. They are recommended on Wall Street. So this really is an attractive investment for both the conservative and opportunistic investor.

D-2. EQUITY MUTUAL FUND

Jonathan Walker (Risk-Averse Expert)—Commentary

It appears that the market is just pausing, instead of being at the end of a rally. Most rallies historically last from eighteen to thirty-six months; this rally has been in effect for only a year. Inflation is stabilizing. Orders and sales are doing well. GNP is up. Spending is not terrible. It looks like unemployment is coming down. The market is the place to be, along with the bulls, when a rally is in session.

Therefore, equity mutual funds represent a good investment at this time. They have the advantages of diversification, professional management, and lower transaction fees. The Atlas Zenith Fund in particular has had an excellent track record. It has grown an average of 16% per year and invests only in the more successful companies in the Fortune 500. It looks like a good bet.

(Continued from page 33)

RESULTS:
C-2. SPREADSHEET $YSTEMS

THE EXPERTS SPEAK
———— Georgina Gold ————

Good move. You rolled with the punches and profited hand-somely. You realized that the public pays dearly for successful new upstarts. Any healthy P/E ratio would generate more cash than corporate bonds ever could, which is exactly what happened. Now is the time when real skills are needed to determine whether or not to stick with a rapidly growing yet risky company.

Rumors are to Wall Street what mosquitoes are to a swamp—they're everywhere and mostly none too helpful, although many creatures live off them. The rumor that Spreadsheet $ystems would go public was true. The rumor that the market would go crazy over it was not true. The computer software industry was having its first sign of problems. Intense competition and other rumors of a possible shakeout caused investors to be wary. So instead of putting you well on your way to becoming a millionaire as you had hoped, the market valued your shares at only 7X earnings. However, since earnings were $1.5 million, the market value of the company was $10.5 million (i.e., $1.5 million times 7). Therefore, your nearly 3% of the company was worth $299,250, which means you made a profit of $117,650. That's pretty good. Moreover, now your shares are liquid and your cup truly runneth over.

You're ecstatic, but what do you do next? You think you've made as much money as you can from Spreadsheet $ystems, and there is little likelihood that this windfall will be repeated. Your ever-optimistic friend from the software company, however, disagrees. He is certain that the company is poised to take off. Top management is very optimistic about the future. After all, who ever heard of anyone not needing help with their finances? You look at the numbers and the projections, and you must admit they don't look bad. More-over, there are now rumors that Spreadsheet Systems will merge with another computer software manufacturer, which would send the price of the stock soaring even further. You only hope that this rumor is true. On the other hand, you can always put your money into the new asset management accounts and move your money when the spirit moves you.

You go over the numbers carefully. After all, the money is your inheritance, and you earned it.

Bank Investment Advisory Newsletter

Recovery from the recession stutters. After a year in which interest and inflation rates steadily declined, both measures of economic vitality took a turn for the worse. Aggravated by a more restrictive money supply, the discount rate increased a full percent. The prime rate rose a point to 13%. Capital spending on plant and equipment likewise has suffered. Consumer spending is expected to decline unless interest rates can be lowered. The real key is inflation. If inflation remains stable at 10% or declines, actions of the Fed are likely to be eased.

Despite high rates, certain segments of the economy held their own. Car sales increased 10% over a year ago. With more people traveling, airlines showed a whopping 20% gain. However, banks and electric utilities remain anemic.

The GNP grew at a slow 2.3% pace. Government spending continues to trouble economists. Leading economic analysts question whether the ever-growing federal deficit can be controlled. Unemployment also remains bleak at 10%. The major question now is whether this halt in the recovery is temporary or whether the three plagues of the recession— high interest rates, high inflation, and high unemployment—have returned to stay.

SPREADSHEET $YSTEMS
CHAIRMAN'S MESSAGE TO SHAREHOLDERS

Computer software sales slumped badly this year to $6,000,000. After two years of rapid growth and expansion, public demand for software has just not kept pace with the supply. Not only are there too many competitors, but the general public's acceptance of the personal computer is taking longer than originally expected.

To maintain profitability within this difficult environment, we have reduced production and administrative expenses. Still, our net income dropped to $750,000. But on a more positive note, we are widely regarded to have the best marketing and distribution staff in the industry. We need talented program designers, and we are currently exploring different avenues in order to acquire them, including merger discussions.

Despite previous problems, we remain optimistic. We fully expect sales to top the $10 million mark and profits to rebound to former levels. Should additional new programs be introduced, we predict even higher sales and net income. Our efforts to attract new designers . . .

DECISION D

The current value of your investment is *$299,250*. Tough luck, your investment is 7% below the average of the experts.

D-3 **Do you stick with Spreadsheet $ystems** and hope the stock takes off amid the merger rumors? (Turn to page 90.)

or

D-4 **Do you sell your shares** at a good profit **and put your money into a conservative asset management account** paying 9%, or $26,933? (Turn to page 95.)

After you have made your decision, turn to the next page for the experts' choices.

THE EXPERTS STRATEGIZE:
D-3. SPREADSHEET $YSTEMS

Georgina Gold (Opportunistic Expert) did not take this alternative.

Smart investing is knowing when to sell. The computer software industry is hurting badly. Sales and profits are down. The company is having problems keeping designers, which is critical to succeeding in this industry. The rumors of merger are very problematic, since who wants to acquire problems? Everyone has enough problems of his own. Now is the time to sell. An asset management account looks like a good and profitable place to be.

D-4. SELL SPREADSHEET $YSTEMS/ ASSET MANAGEMENT ACCOUNT

Georgina Gold (Opportunistic Expert) took this alternative.

I made my money when Spreadsheet $ystems went public, and now is the time to consolidate my holdings in an asset management account. I'll get a very safe return on my investment while I investigate other alternatives. The economy is pausing, and this is the time to wait for a clear signal to emerge. There always will be other opportunities. Spreadsheet $ystems is not in a high-growth position, so I will hold my money and wait for something better to come along—like Spreadsheet $ystems a year ago.

(Continued from page 37)

RESULTS:
C-3. OPTIONS/TIME DEPOSITS

THE EXPERTS SPEAK
———————————— Jonathan Walker ————————————

After two years you finally tried something a bit risky and got burned. So much for living dangerously. The problem is that options are major league investments and you are a minor league player. Options are difficult to make money on, although they do offer the potential for sizeable rewards. For starters, however, you might want to try something a little simpler and a little less risky. When you have a lot of money to throw away, try options again.

Although you have had your inheritance for only two years, already you're acting like a longtime investor. So get ready to take your lumps like one of the big boys (or girls). The blue-chip company, American Diversified Industries, increased sales, profits, and market share 20%. While the stock went up, it did not appreciate enough for you to make a profit on your option. Luckily, since your options still had some time before they lapsed, you were able to sell them for what you paid for them. However, because you didn't earn interest on them for a year, you really lost money.

Nevertheless, all is not lost, since you made 11%, or nearly $7,200, on the $65,378 you put into time deposits. Your banker's husband, Nathaniel, the financial savant, still feels that American Diversified Industries is poised for explosive growth. Therefore, he advises you to renew your options. That piece of advice and 50¢ will buy you a cup of coffee. Still, you're willing to look at the numbers.

You also decide you want something safe but with a good return. Nathaniel, sensing a possible lost account, quickly touts T bills as the greatest invention since the knife and fork. T bills are direct obligations of the federal government that are issued with a maturity of one year or less. They're safe, backed by the full faith and obligation of the U.S. government. Unless you're a socialist, what more could you want?

You feel better, but still you want to look at the economic data to see what the future portends.

Bank Investment Advisory Newsletter

Recovery from the recession stutters. After a year in which interest and inflation rates steadily declined, both measures of economic vitality took a turn for the worse. Aggravated by a more restrictive money supply, the discount rate increased a full percent. The prime rate rose a point to 13%. Capital spending on plant and equipment likewise has suffered. Consumer spending is expected to decline unless interest rates can be lowered. The real key is inflation. If inflation remains stable at 10% or declines, actions of the Fed are likely to be eased.

Despite high rates, certain segments of the economy held their own. Car sales increased 10% over a year ago. With more people traveling, airlines showed a whopping 20% gain. However, banks and electric utilities remain anemic.

The GNP grew at a slow 2.3% pace. Government spending continues to trouble economists. Leading economic analysts question whether the ever-growing federal deficit can be controlled. Unemployment also remains bleak at 10%. The major question now is whether this halt in the recovery is temporary or whether the three plagues of the recession—high interest rates, high inflation, and high unemployment—have returned to stay.

Street Scene Magazine

"TEMPORARILY DISCONNECTED—NOW BACK ON-LINE"

American Diversified Industries is a highly diversified company. Growth in revenues and profits has been excellent, 20% in the last year. American Diversified Industries is also well positioned to take advantage of growing markets in the major areas of operation, especially fast food and financial services. Revenues in these areas grew 50% and 40%, respectively. Total revenues for the company are now $600 million, with net income of $45 million after an extraordinary write-off for sales of the phone equipment line.

Unable to hook up enough subscribers to make any money, the telephone subsidiary did not achieve profitability. In a highly competitive marketplace, this marketing failure put a squeeze on profit margins. Moreover, it diverted the energies of the CEO and his staff to try to turn the business around.

The divestiture of the phone lines should enable top management to devote more time to managing growth areas. The one note of caution has been a concern that top management still is being stretched too thin to adequately control widely diverse and growing industries. Still, the stock is recommended because revenues and profits should grow—American Diversified seems to be in the right place at the right time with the right product.

DECISION D

The current value of your investment is *$137,948.* Tough luck, your investment is 57% below the average of the experts.

D-5   *Do you put your faith, prayers (it's only in God we trust), and money in government T bills* paying 9.5%, or $13,105? (Turn to page 98.)

or

D-6   *Do you continue to keep your money tied up in options and time deposits* in the hope of making a killing? (Turn to page 102.)

After you have made your decision, see the next page for the experts' comments.

THE EXPERTS STRATEGIZE:
D-5. T BILLS

Jonathan Walker (Risk-Averse Expert)—Commentary

T bills are absolutely the safest investment to put your money into. There is no risk on the principal. Your interest will be paid by the U.S. government. This is the place to put money when you don't really know what you want to do with it, yet you want to make sure you have it when you want it. Money can be withdrawn from T bills at any time. The markets are extremely liquid.

D-6. OPTIONS/TIME DEPOSITS

Georgina Gold (Opportunistic Expert)—Commentary

This is an interesting mix. You have a great deal of risk with options, although you are buying options in a company that seems to have a superior growth record. In time deposits there is no risk at all. Thus, the entire investment is not quite as risky as it would at first appear because you are diversifying your earnings stream, or the amount of money you earn. However, the money invested in options still is highly exposed, and the killing you hope to make could result in your being killed instead.

(Continued from page 37)

RESULTS:
C-4. TIME DEPOSITS

THE EXPERTS SPEAK
Jonathan Walker

True to form, you stayed conservative and made a decent return. It was a smart move given that the alternative, options, was risky in an economy that's not great. As long as the economy remains sluggish, a risk-averse strategy is good. The only problem is that you'll never get rich that way either. *Que será, será.*

Your conservative stripes are showing. Your decision to invest in time deposits is wise, although not too imaginative. You did earn $14,383 on your $131,000 investment, and with very little risk involved. As long as interest rates remain high, you can continue to earn a double-digit return. Not bad.

On the other hand, maybe there's more to life than clipping 20¢-off coupons, driving a ten-year-old car, and investing in time deposits. You call the banker's husband Nathaniel and explain the dilemma. You want a higher return without unconscionable risk. He says you've asked him a very tough one (as if you had asked him to explain the meaning of truth, beauty, and life). Still, Nathaniel feels there is an investment which meets these objectives. Why not buy a stock market index fund either of the Fortune 500 or the Dow Jones Averages? If the combined price (the averages) goes up, you make that percentage. If it goes down—well there are always money market funds. Assuming you pick a relatively safe or high-quality index fund and the recent gains in the bull market continue, you should make money. While last year the Fortune 500 and Dow Jones indexes gained only 6% and 8%, respectively, that was during a recession. Great things are expected now.

This stock market index fund doesn't sound bad at all. You get to play the market with a more limited risk. You put your prognostication hat on, look at the bank's monthly newsletter, and then decide.

Bank Investment Advisory Newsletter

Recovery from the recession stutters. After a year in which interest and inflation rates steadily declined, both measures of economic vitality took a turn for the worse. Aggravated by a more restrictive money supply, the discount rate increased a full percent. The prime rate rose a point to 13%. Capital spending on plant and equipment likewise has suffered. Consumer spending is expected to decline unless interest rates can be lowered. The real key is inflation. If inflation remains stable at 10% or declines, actions of the Fed are likely to be eased.

Despite high rates, certain segments of the economy held their own. Car sales increased 10% over a year ago. With more people traveling, airlines showed a whopping 20% gain. However, banks and electric utilities remain anemic.

The GNP grew at a slow 2.3% pace. Government spending continues to trouble economists. Leading economic analysts question whether the ever-growing federal deficit can be controlled. Unemployment also remains bleak at 10%. The major question now is whether this halt in the recovery is temporary or whether the three plagues of the recession—high interest rates, high inflation, and high unemployment—have returned to stay.

T. KITZINGER'S MARKET OUTLOOK

The market has remained strong despite the stuttering economy. It is generally felt on Wall Street that the current aberrations are only temporary and that the economy will pick up in the next few months. The fact that car sales and travel showed vitality indicates that consumers have not lost faith in the recovery.

Activity on the Street remains brisk. Volume is heavy, with Dow Jones Averages showing strong gains (6% over the past two months). The Dow Jones is expected to continue strong as long as the economy shapes up as predicted.

DECISION D

The current value of your investment is *$145,139.* Tough luck, your investment is 55% below the average of the experts.

D-7 ***Do you keep your money in absolutely, positively safe time deposits*** paying 11%, or $15,965? (Turn to page 106.)

or

D-8 ***Do you pick the stock market index fund*** (Dow Jones Averages) in the hope of riding the bull market up without getting thrown for a loss? (Turn to page 110.)

After you have made your decision, see the next page for the experts' choices.

THE EXPERTS STRATEGIZE: D-7. TIME DEPOSITS

Jonathan Walker (Risk-Averse Expert) took this alternative.

Time deposits are preferable to the stock market index only because the index can go down as well as up. Even though the index has been going up for the last year, it appears that the recovery from the recession is starting to slow down a bit. Capital spending has suffered. Consumer spending is expected to go down. Interest rates are up. As a conservative investor, I would rather not be in the stock market at this time.

I chose time deposits because they are a very safe investment earning a decent rate of return. In addition, I can get my money any time I want it. There's nothing wrong with getting 11% with no risk.

D-8. DOW JONES INDEX FUND

Jonathan Walker (Risk-Averse Expert) did not take this alternative.

The economy looks bad. The recession is stuttering along with high interest rates, high inflation, and high unemployment. This index could easily decline 10% to 15% over the course of a year. It would take me a year to make up that much money. I don't want to risk it in the indices without being paid the proper premium.

(Continued from page 41)

RESULTS:
C-5. SPREADSHEET $YSTEMS SELL-OFF/ASSET MANAGEMENT ACCOUNT

THE EXPERTS SPEAK
Chat Morton

Why? Why? Why? You invested in the company at the beginning. You have seen it through good times. The company appeared on the verge of becoming highly profitable for everyone connected with it. Why change? The public is looking for any companies which end in *x* or *onics* and generally is willing to pay a healthy premium for owning them (10X to 20X earnings). Even a small multiple times earnings returns better money than you made. Bad move.

So you decided to sell. Take the money and run. You figured you had made money investing in Spreadsheet $ystems and now was the time to look elsewhere. Smart move? Well, Spreadsheet $ystems went public as rumored, and public reception was less than enthusiastic. In fact, concern over an increasingly crowded field and possible shakeout caused the market to pay a small premium (7X earnings) for the new stock. However, since earnings were $1.5 million and you owned 5% of the company, a 7X multiple was worth $525,000, or almost $175,000 more than what you made in selling before the public offering. You took the sure thing and lost. Well, not exactly—you still made over $110,000 and your investment is worth over $350,000. You are not unhappy, just a bit wistful. You could have been even richer.

Still, you are rich, and you need help. You call up Leonard, your cousin who also is a financial advisor. While he's barely talked to you in the past, now he acts and talks as if he were your best friend. In fact, he loves you like a broker. (And you thought a dog was man's best friend.) With your income, Leonard recommends tax-free municipals. He explains these are debt obligations of nonfederal governmental units, which are not taxable at the federal and sometimes even the state and local levels. The larger your income, the more advantageous they become. While the after-tax interest rate is a low 7%, the pre-tax equivalent rate is 11.6%. If you put your funds into municipals, your investment will increase by $40,730 on a pretax equivalent basis. In addition, since these munis are highly rated by Moody's (Aa) they are very safe.

If you want more return (with obviously greater risk), Leonard suggests a combination of munis—for safety and income—and stock options—for upside growth. For a small fee you can purchase stock options. If the stock price goes above the exercise price plus the fee within a specified period of time, then you make money. For example, if the exercise price is $105, and the fee is $5, and the stock is currently selling for $100, then the price of the stock would have to increase more than $10 for you to make a profit. Simple. Leonard suggests options on a new high-tech company, Light Sat, Inc., which is "primed to take off."

You're enough of an expert now to say "let's look at the numbers."

Bank Investment Advisory Newsletter

Recovery from the recession stutters. After a year in which interest and inflation rates steadily declined, both measures of economic vitality took a turn for the worse. Aggravated by a more restrictive money supply, the discount rate increased a full percent. The prime rate rose a point to 13%. Capital spending on plant and equipment likewise has suffered. Consumer spending is expected to decline unless interest rates can be lowered. The real key is inflation. If inflation remains stable at 10% or declines, actions of the Fed are likely to be eased.

Despite high rates, certain segments of the economy held their own. Car sales increased 10% over a year ago. With more people traveling, airlines showed a whopping 20% gain. However, banks and electric utilities remain anemic.

The GNP grew at a slow 2.3% pace. Government spending continues to trouble economists. Leading economic analysts question whether the ever-growing federal deficit can be controlled. Unemployment also remains bleak at 10%. The major question now is whether this halt in the recovery is temporary or whether the three plagues of the recession—high interest rates, high inflation, and high unemployment—have returned to stay.

MERIT-PYNCH INVESTMENT REPORT

LIGHT SAT, INC.

Light Sat, Inc., a manufacturer of small commercial satellites, has built a number of prototypes which are designed to bring space to the average company. It is the most technologically advanced company of its kind in the field.

Light Sat was started three years ago by three engineers from Boeing. They raised $100 million on an initial public offering. The stock was offered at $20 a share, rose to $50 a share, and has since dropped back to $30. During the first three years the company reported losses of $25, $15, and $5 million dollars. The company is now ready to begin manufacture of its first truly commercial satellite. If the satellite is a success, it should generate large sums of money. Since only a prototype has been developed, this house considers the investment risky.

DECISION D

The current value of your investment is *$351,120*. Congratulations, your investment is 9% above the average of the experts.

D-9   *Do you invest in 7% tax-free munis* (11.6% pre-tax equivalent) like the other rich investors? (Turn to page 114.)

or

D-10   *Do you go for a combination of growth (options) with safety (municipal bonds)?* (Turn to page 119.)

After you have made your decision, turn to the next page for the experts' comments.

THE EXPERTS STRATEGIZE:
D-9. TAX-FREE MUNICIPALS

Jonathan Walker (Risk-Averse Expert)—Commentary

Why would anyone choose to pay taxes. The 7% tax-free income is very good. The bonds are safe and can easily be bought and sold. The primary disadvantage is that if interest rates go up, the value of the bonds goes down, because your money could be earning more elsewhere. Therefore, the bonds are worth less if you try to sell them as compared to what you could make on another investment. But in any case, the guaranteed pre-tax equivalent yield still is over 11%, year after year. A very safe and wise investment for the cautious at heart.

D-10. OPTIONS/MUNICIPALS

Chat Morton (High-Risk Expert)—Commentary

This is a very good mix. Light Sat has an interesting product that could really fly. The product is useful and needed. Whether it will work and the company make money from it are other questions. Still, it is worth considering. If half the money is put into relatively safe tax-free municipals, the rest can be used to roll the dice. There's a nice complementary aspect to this investment strategy, which offers both safety and upside potential.

(Continued from page 41)

RESULTS:
C-6. SPREADSHEET $YSTEMS

THE EXPERTS SPEAK
Chat Morton

Savvy. The company went public and you did very well. While you did not make as much as you had hoped, in three years you've increased your inheritance to over half a million dollars. Successful new companies with good track records are rare. Therefore, when you find one, stick with it. The economics are such that even when low multiples of earnings are paid for new companies, original investors can make a lot of money.

You bet on the company. It had everything going for it: successful products, good management, a growing market, a good track record, and a good future. Management believed in the company enough to attempt to buy back the stock at a healthy 33% premium. You hoped to become an instant millionaire. However, the market saw other signals as well—intense competition, a possible shakeout, and delayed introduction of the company's new financial programs. Hence, when the stock went public, the market paid only 7X earning. Nevertheless, since earnings were $1.5 million and you owned 5% of the company, you made almost $300,000. Moreover, now you can easily sell your shares anytime you want to, since the stock is publicly traded.

Maybe that's what you should do—sell your stock. You made a lot of money when the company went public, and now you wonder whether you should cash in on your bonanza. Your friend from the company tells you definitely not to sell your shares. The company is thinking of merging with another computer software company. Great upside potential. You think of the old saying—two heads are better than none. It's worth considering. The Spreadsheet Systems investment has been good to you.

Still, maybe you should consider other investment opportunities. You flip through the Yellow Pages looking for investment expertise (isn't that how everyone does it?). You find the nationwide, easily recognizable firm of Theodore & Assoc. You call up and Mr. Theodore himself answers. He listens to your story and without hesitation recommends tax-free municipal mutual funds to someone in your situation. These are funds comprised of debt obligations of nonfederal governmental authorities, which are not taxed at the federal and sometimes the state and local levels. Municipals have the primary advantage, unlike most other investments, of being tax-free. It just so happens his firm has put together just such a fund paying 8%, which when adjusted for tax consequences yields the equivalent of 13.3%.

You think your money would be safer in mutual funds, but still, Spreadsheet Systems has turned you on. A brief look at the investment newsletter and other financial data should provide guidance, which, along with prayer, is the basis of all good investment decision making.

Bank Investment Advisory Newsletter

Recovery from the recession stutters. After a year in which interest and inflation rates steadily declined, both measures of economic vitality took a turn for the worse. Aggravated by a more restrictive money supply, the discount rate increased a full percent. The prime rate rose a point to 13%. Capital spending on plant and equipment likewise has suffered. Consumer spending is expected to decline unless interest rates can be lowered. The real key is inflation. If inflation remains stable at 10% or declines, actions of the Fed are likely to be eased.

Despite high rates, certain segments of the economy held their own. Car sales increased 10% over a year ago. With more people traveling, airlines showed a whopping 20% gain. However, banks and electric utilities remain anemic.

The GNP grew at a slow 2.3% pace. Government spending continues to trouble economists. Leading economic analysts question whether the ever-growing federal deficit can be controlled. Unemployment also remains bleak at 10%. The major question now is whether this halt in the recovery is temporary or whether the three plagues of the recession—high interest rates, high inflation, and high unemployment—have returned to stay.

SPREADSHEET $YSTEMS
CHAIRMAN'S MESSAGE TO SHAREHOLDERS

Computer software sales slumped badly this year to $6,000,000. After two years of rapid growth and expansion, public demand for software has just not kept pace with the ever-growing supply. Not only are there too many competitors, but the general public's acceptance of personal computers is taking longer than originally expected.

To maintain profitability within this difficult environment, we have reduced production and administrative expenses. Still, our net income dropped to $750,000. But on a more positive note, we are widely regarded to have the best marketing and distribution staff in the industry. We need talented program designers, and we are currently exploring different avenues in order to acquire them, including merger discussions.

Despite previous problems, we remain optimistic. We fully expect sales to top the $10 million mark and profits to rebound to former levels. Should additional new programs be introduced, we predict even higher sales and net income. Our efforts to attract new designers . . .

DECISION D

The current value of your investment is $525,000. Congratulations, your investment is 62% above the average of the experts.

D-11 *Do you continue to stay with Spreadsheet $ystems,* with visions of a merger dancing in your head? (Turn to page 122.)

or

D-12 *Do you switch to a tax-free municipal mutual fund* paying 13.3%, or $69,825 (pre-tax equivalent), and count the interest daily? (Turn to page 126.)

After you have made your decision, turn to the next page for the experts' choices.

THE EXPERTS STRATEGIZE:
D-11. SPREADSHEET $YSTEMS

Chat Morton (High-Risk Expert) took this alternative.

I'm a roller, and I'm going to play this out. There's no point in getting off the ship now because it looks like it's coming into port. Even though sales and profits are down, there are merger rumors. I could make a lot of money if someone comes in and pays me a big premium over the market, so I will choose this instead of the munis. If you're weak at heart, you shouldn't play this game. Luckily, I've had a transplant and I'm ready to go.

D-12. MUNICIPAL MUTUAL FUND

Chat Morton (High-Risk Expert) did not take this alternative.

Munis are for old folk. I'm never going to get rich earning a pre-tax equivalent yield of 13.3%. I'm an American. I want to make enough so I can pay a lot of taxes. I'm almost thirty years old. I want to live a little bit. If I lose it, I lose it. Munis are just not my style at this point.

(Continued from page 46)

RESULTS:
C-7. SHORT-TERM BOND FUND

THE EXPERTS SPEAK
——————— Jonathan Walker ———————

Okay. As long as you continue to get middle range double-digit yields, there is no reason to look elsewhere. The economy is just beginning to pick up. This means that until the recovery is more definite, other opportunities may be risky. Therefore, debt obligations or bonds of good corporations make a lot of dollars and cents.

Why gamble if you can make 14% relatively safely? Your money will double in only five years. It's hard to beat the 14% return you got from the short-term bond fund. Your investment increased by \$32,172. However, making money is like making love—all good things must come to an end. As interest rates have fallen, so has the yield of the bond fund. It is now 11%. You will now have to work to make additional dollars.

You seek your cousin Leonard's advice. He says there is no way to make 14% in this market, unless you begin to speculate a bit. Recognizing your desire for some safety and security, he recommends switching to a mutual fund that invests in high fliers and offers a variable rate. Although you are playing the market, with a mutual fund you minimize the risk of being wiped out by a single bad investment. At the same time, your upside potential is also limited. He suggests buying a fund called the High-Tech Group, which has done very well in the past. While there is no rate guarantee, this high-flier fund has consistently been paying almost 15% per year.

If you are unsure of what you want to do, says Leonard, maybe the best thing to do is put the money in a money market fund. With the economy improving, you could earn decent interest yet still take advantage of other opportunities that arise.

You need to consolidate your new-found fortune. The question is how. You read the reports and decide.

Bank Investment Advisory Newsletter

Recovery from the recession stutters. After a year in which interest and inflation rates steadily declined, both measures of economic vitality took a turn for the worse. Aggravated by a more restrictive money supply, the discount rate increased a full percent. The prime rate rose a point to 13%. Capital spending on plant and equipment likewise has suffered. Consumer spending is expected to decline unless interest rates can be lowered. The real

---

key is inflation. If inflation remains stable at 10% or declines, actions of the Fed are likely to be eased.

Despite high rates, certain segments of the economy held their own. Car sales increased 10% over a year ago. With more people traveling, airlines showed a whopping 20% gain. However, banks and electric utilities remain anemic.

The GNP grew at a slow 2.3% pace. Government spending continues to trouble economists. Leading economic analysts question whether the ever-growing federal deficit can be controlled. Unemployment also remains bleak at 10%. The major question now is whether this halt in the recovery is temporary or whether the three plagues of the recession—high interest rates, high inflation, and high unemployment—have returned to stay.

MERIT-PYNCH INVESTMENT REPORT

THE HIGH-TECH GROUP MUTUAL FUND

The High-Tech Group invests in leading-edge technology companies which must meet very stringent financial and growth criteria, including initial capitalization of $50 million or more and market growth potential of 20% or more per year. As a result, in the past three years, the High-Tech Group has done well investing in laser optics, bioengineering, and computer simulation companies. The fund has consistently returned 15% or more per year and in some years up to 35%. Among the funds which invest in this area, the High-Tech Group is one of the top performers, as rated by *Money* magazine.

A word of caution is necessary. Since the High-Tech Group invests in new technology, the possibility always exists that the technology will not succeed or be accepted. While recent purchases have been successful, new technology still is considered to be highly risky.

DECISION D

The current value of your investment is *$261,972*. Tough luck, your investment is 19% below the average of the experts.

D-13 *Do you stay conservative and continue with the money market fund* paying 11%, or $28,817? (Turn to page 132.)

or

D-14 *Do you gamble on high-flier mutual funds,* which have done well in the past (Turn to page 136.)

After you have made your decision, turn to the next page for the experts' comments.

THE EXPERTS STRATEGIZE:
D-13. MONEY MARKET FUND

Jonathan Walker (Risk-Averse Expert)—Commentary

This fund is diversified in a wide variety of large international banks. There is not much risk because all the CDs from these banks are short-term and the managers of these funds are keeping on top of which countries and which banks may be exhibiting signs of trouble. Not only is it relatively risk-free, it also is better than can be done investing domestically.

D-14. HIGH-TECH MUTUAL FUND

Chat Morton (High-Risk Expert)—Commentary

The high-flying mutual fund is a high-technology fund. The game in this case is the ability to continue to identify growing companies that are not going to get blown out in an industry shakeout. Not all these companies can continue to grow at 20% to 25% a year. Mathematically, it is impossible, so at some point in time there will be a retrenchment. It is critical to be able to count on managers who identify the good companies, hit the good niches, and then get out of the companies as the growth curves begin to level out and the industry becomes congested. This fund has been able to do this in the past. However, the future is a whole new ball game.

(Continued from page 46)

RESULTS:
C-8. GRAIN FUTURES

THE EXPERTS SPEAK
———————— **Georgina Gold** ————————

Big deal. You took a chance and lost. Nobody wins all the time. Still, you should look for investments with better odds.

Two of the three investments you made so far, the new company and this one, really could be classified as high-risk. Luckily, you made money on one. Most investors don't make anything supplying venture capital or buying commodities. Unless you plan to become more proficient (and with your track record it is highly unlikely), I would look carefully before investing in any more risky alternatives.

You should have listened to your cousin Leonard. Grain futures are not the place for those who hope to make a lot of bread all the time with little dough. Only the rich can survive the vicissitudes of the commodities market, which, unfortunately, went down. While you did not lose all your money, only 25%, you didn't make any either. Your opportunity costs (what you would have made in a money market fund) plus your loss in commodities equals a 40% drop in the value of your investment. Nobody's perfect.

You call up your cousin Leonard, the financial advisor. He says don't worry, it's only money. Comforting thoughts from someone who makes money regardless of whether or not you do. The problem with grain futures, he says, is they are too abstract and unpredictable. Therefore, why not buy gold futures? Leonard predicts the price of gold will rise, since in general the interest rates are falling (despite a temporary rise) and the world situation is horrible. At the first sign of bad news, the price of gold should skyrocket. That makes you feel very good.

However, instead of putting all your money into gold futures, he suggests that you put part of your money into blue-chip corporate bonds, which are as solid as the Rock of Gibraltar. This should prevent another 25% wipeout. On the other hand, if you want to be completely safe, Leonard advises that you put all your funds into corporate bonds paying 10%.

You want to be safe but not sorry. Maybe the gold futures/bond combination is right. Let's see what direction you can glean from the economic newsletter.

Bank Investment Advisory Newsletter

Recovery from the recession stutters. After a year in which interest and inflation rates steadily declined, both measures of economic vitality took a turn for the worse. Aggravated by a more restrictive money supply, the discount rate increased a full percent. The prime rate rose a point to 13%. Capital spending on plant and equipment likewise has suffered. Consumer spending is expected to decline unless interest rates can be lowered. The real key is inflation. If inflation remains stable at 10% or declines, actions of the Fed are likely to be eased.

Despite high rates, certain segments of the economy held their own. Car sales increased 10% over a year ago. With more people traveling, airlines showed a whopping 20% gain. However, banks and electric utilities remain anemic.

The GNP grew at a slow 2.3% pace. Government spending continues to trouble economists. Leading economic analysts question whether the ever-growing federal deficit can be controlled. Unemployment also remains bleak at 10%. The major question now is whether this halt in the recovery is temporary or whether the three plagues of the recession—high interest rates, high inflation, and high unemployment—have returned to stay

PRECIOUS METTLE □ □ □
An investment analysis □ □

THE FUTURE OF GOLD

Gold is viewed as a good investment for the next six to nine months. After peaking in 1979, the price of gold has fallen to new lows below $400. We believe that the price has bottomed out and that investors will seek to make a quick profit on the undervalued metal. In addition, new gold discoveries in Canada and the Soviet Union have not turned out to be as extensive as originally estimated, which should further inflate the price of gold. Foreign unrest in Africa and the Middle East continues to trouble investors, who we predict will look to gold for security in a troubled world . . .

DECISION D

The current value of your investment is *$172,350*. Tough luck, your investment is 47% below the average of the experts.

D-15 **Do you put all your money into safe blue-chip bonds** paying 10%, or $17,235? (Turn to page 140.)

or

D-16 **Do you** get gold fever and **put part of your money in gold futures and the rest in corporate bonds?** (Turn to page 146.)

After you have made your decision, turn to the next page for the experts' comments.

THE EXPERTS STRATEGIZE:
D-15. CORPORATE BONDS

Jonathan Walker (Risk-Averse Expert)—Commentary

Corporate bonds typically are very safe. They are debt with a senior claim on a company's assets if the company develops any problems. The 10% interest is good. The only risk is if interest rates go up sharply, the price of the bonds will drop. It is possible to reduce this risk by buying shorter term bonds.

The economy seems to favor an investment of this type. Inflation is falling, which should help interest rates. As a result, in the near term there should be little principal risk.

D-16. GOLD FUTURES/CORPORATE BONDS

Georgina Gold (Opportunistic Expert)—Commentary

Gold traditionally has been an investment for the pessimist. When there is war, disaster, famine, or floods, the price of gold tends to respond positively. However, it is very difficult to know where gold is going to go, because no one can accurately predict the future. In addition, supply and demand are unstable. South Africa could sell less gold than the demand, driving the price up. Gold futures are even more risky, because you put up only a fraction of the amount of the underlying gold you control, which means you could suffer extremely large losses (or benefit from very large gains). Any way you look at it, it is a risky investment.

(Continued from page 51)

RESULTS:
D-1. CONVERTIBLE DEBENTURES

THE EXPERTS SPEAK
—————————— Chat Morton ——————————

You've taken small risks so far in real estate and convertible bonds and received small rewards. You're not starving, and your capital has grown to almost $225,000. Not enough to retire on, but enough to feel a bit independent. With the economy improving, Current Technologies could benefit from a healthy, growing marketplace. Therefore, it makes sense to continue to invest in the electrical company. Eventually risks do pay off (unless you are quite unlucky).

Before you started to learn something about investing, you thought a convertible debenture was something you slept on. Now you know it's another place besides the mattress where you can put your money. Regardless, you made a wise decision.

Current Technologies, that well-known manufacturer of electrical products, is having a great year and is a favorite on Wall Street. Sales were up 15% while profits climbed a whopping 30%. A combination of new products, growing markets, and strong cost controls augur an even brighter future. The market, sensing even greater profits, has pushed the stock up 13% over a year ago. As a result, the value of your bond rose 4% in addition to the 7% interest you made. All totaled, your investment increased 11%, or $22,176. Not too shabby.

Now you wonder whether to keep the convertible bond or to sell it at a profit and buy a corporate note with a guaranteed interest rate. You call up Nathaniel, and he says it's a tough call. You compliment him on being a master of the obvious and ask what he recommends. He suggests holding the debenture and taking a chance with the high-flying blue-chip

electrical giant, because the company is a winner. You remember that you got out just in time from your last "winner,"
Spreadsheet Systems, which now makes International Har-
vester look like a great buy. You review the papers and decide.

Bank Investment Advisory Newsletter

The economy is on a roll again as the recovery returns. Consumer
prices increased only .7% last month, for an annual rate of 8%.
The prime rate dropped 1% to 12%. Unemployment declined for
the first time in recent memory, to 9%. At the same time the GNP
grew at a 6% annualized rate. A host of industries are participating
in this turnaround. Car manufacturers, oil companies, and electric
utilities reported larger-than-average gains both in unit and dollar
volume. Retail sales reported a strong fourth quarter as shoppers
flocked to X-mas stores for pre- and post-sales. Even housing demand, pent up for some time, showed some vigor. Housing starts
were up 5%.

The index of leading economic indicators was up. Led by stock
prices, new orders for consumer goods and materials, and building
permits, the index rose 6% versus a year ago. Government spending was also stable, as military spending slowed for the first time
in two years. All indicators point to continued improvement for
the economy.

Street Scene Magazine

"UP, UP, AND AWAY"

. . . Some things never change. Current Technologies increased its sales from $6 billion to $6.9 billion with profits climbing an impressive $100 million. Especially strong performance was recorded in the consumer and new products area. The company seems to have an inexhaustible supply of great ideas . . . Since the P/E ratio of 10.3 is only slightly above the industry average, the stock remains a strong "buy" recommendation of the major brokerage houses.

. . . The only note of caution is the increased competition in the consumer area from cheaper Far Eastern imports. Top management from Current Technologies has not expressed great concern because . . .

DECISION E

The current value of your investment is *$223,780.* Tough luck, your investment is 26% below the average of the experts.

E-1 **Do you keep the debenture,** anticipating big gains from the blue-chip giant? (Turn to page 149.)

or

E-2 **Do you continue to protect your investment by selling the bond** at a profit **and reinvesting in an 11% corporate note,** which would yield $24,616? (Turn to page 153.)

After you have made your decision, turn to the next page for the experts' comments.

THE EXPERTS STRATEGIZE: E-1. CONVERTIBLE BONDS

Georgina Gold (Opportunistic Expert)—Commentary

Convertible bonds have two main advantages: a guaranteed yield, which makes it like a bond, but also an upside potential should the stock rally. Current Technologies is a good-looking stock. Sales and profits are up. Growth is coming from new products and markets, while costs are being controlled. What more could you want? In this case, there are good upside possibilities in terms of bond appreciation, while the bond yield will protect you on the downside.

E-2. SELL DEBENTURES/BUY CORPORATE NOTE

Jonathan Walker (Risk-Averse Expert)—Commentary

Corporate notes provide a senior call on the assets of the company. This is a very safe investment, on the low end of the risk spectrum. It also provides a low yet safe interest rate. Typically, notes are shorter term (one year or less), which reduces the risk of interest rates going up, thereby eroding investment principal. Nonetheless, an investment of this type does not reflect a great deal of imagination or adventure in your soul.

(Continued from page 51)

RESULTS: D-2. EQUITY MUTUAL FUND

THE EXPERTS SPEAK
Chat Morton

To you, caution is next to God. Except for real estate, all your investments have been relatively risk-free. You have done well. The problem is you will probably have to live like a saint since you haven't made enough money to splurge. The economy is on the move. Interest rates are down. Consumer spending and GNP are up. Maybe now is the time to throw caution to the winds.

A risk taker you're not. Gambling to you means seeing a new movie only after you have read three favorable reviews and heard two personal recommendations from people who have seen it. Even the name of the mutual fund you selected, the Atlas Zenith Fund, suggests high, strong performance. By only investing in well-established but innovative companies, the fund has earned its name. This year is no exception. The fund returned 13%, which, given your $201,000 investment, meant a $26,000 gain. Not bad. Not bad at all.

However, you begin to wonder if that's enough. To some people, making money is like making love—there's never enough. To others, 13% is okay. You're young, ambitious, and almost rich. You want to make a fortune and appear on the cover of *Money* magazine. Nothing is impossible for you.

You call up Nathaniel and tell him you want to see him immediately if not sooner. Minutes later, he arrives. You explain that you're ready to play craps. What does he recommend? If you're serious, he says, the ultimate risk is penny stocks. Traded on the Denver Stock Exchange, penny stocks offer you the ability to buy large numbers of shares cheaply in hopes that some will pay off. It's always easier to earn a greater percentage on a smaller base. It's also easier to be wiped out. Nathaniel advises that you put half your money in four penny stock mining companies recommended in the *Penny Stock Gazette* and the other half in safe, 6% (10% pre-tax equivalent) munis. If any of the penny stocks strikes the mother lode, you could own *Money* magazine. Of course there is always the possibility (and it's a big one) that the companies could come up empty handed—and that's exactly what your investment would be worth. As an alternative, there are safe, 9% T bills should you decide to continue to be a seat belt investor. T bills, Nathaniel says, are one of the safest investments you can make since they are direct obligations of the U.S. government and are guaranteed by it.

You're indecisive. Maybe the monthly newsletter or the *Penny Stock Gazette* will help.

Bank Investment Advisory Newsletter

The economy is on a roll again as the recovery returns. Consumer prices increased only .7% last month, for an annual rate of 8%. The prime rate dropped 1% to 12%. Unemployment declined for the first time in recent memory, to 9%. At the same time the GNP grew at a 6% annualized rate. A host of industries are participating in this turnaround. Car manufacturers, oil companies, and electric utilities reported larger-than-average gains both in unit and dollar volume. Retail sales reported a strong fourth quarter as shoppers flocked to X-mas stores for pre- and post-sales. Even housing demand, pent up for some time, showed some vigor. Housing starts were up 5%.

The index of leading economic indicators was up. Led by stock prices, new orders for consumer goods and materials, and building permits, the index rose 6% versus a year ago. Government spending was also stable, as military spending slowed for the first time in two years. All indicators point to continued improvement for the economy.

PENNY STOCK GAZETTE

MINING COMPANIES

Mining stocks are highly sought after these days after the Deep Pockets Company discovered gold in the Yukon. Before the discovery the stock had traded at $1.35 a share. After the find, the stock price increased thirtyfold to $40.50. There are a lot of new mining companies, but this letter recommends four which seem to have more experience and potential: CanMine, Inc., Jones Drilling, Hurwitz Bros., and ABD Company. Revenues of each are small at present, but each has acquired mining rights to vast tracts of land near the Deep Pockets find . . .

DECISION E

The current value of your investment is $227,813. Tough luck, your investment is 25% below the average of the experts.

E-3 *Do you continue to go for safety above yield and buy 9% T bills*, returning $20,503? (Turn to page 158.)

or

E-4 *Do you go for the gold, silver, and uranium of the penny stocks with the 6% munis as backup?* (Turn to page 162.)

After you have made your decision, turn to the next page for the experts' comments.

THE EXPERTS STRATEGIZE:
E-3. T BILLS

Jonathan Walker (Risk-Averse Expert)—Commentary

T bills are absolutely the safest investment to put your money into. There is no risk on the principal. Your interest will be paid by the U.S. government. This is the place to put money when you don't really know what you want to do with it, yet you want to make sure you have it when you want it. Money can be withdrawn from T bills at any time. The markets are extremely liquid.

E-4. PENNY MINING STOCKS/MUNIS

Georgina Gold (Opportunistic Expert)—Commentary

Penny mining stocks entail a great deal of risk. You are buying equity in companies which are undercapitalized because it is difficult to raise funds. As a result, the chances of success are small. Penny stocks are very similar to the lottery. Maybe only one in a thousand will hit it big. Most of the others will probably go bankrupt, so you could conceivably lose your entire investment.

(Continued from Page 55)

RESULTS:
D-3. SPREADSHEET $YSTEMS

THE EXPERTS SPEAK
—————————— Chat Morton ——————————

You can't win them all. After making money on time deposits, real estate, and Spreadsheet $ystems, your "luck" ran out. However, there were signs of potential problems that you ignored. The industry was having its share of difficulties, e.g., extreme competition and lowered public demand. The company was having a hard time remaining profitable. Moreover, no new programs were announced. Given these red flags, you should have bailed out. But then again, this is ex post facto advice—which is never wrong.

There are people who make their fortunes on bad news— liquidators and newscasters, for instance. Unfortunately, you are not one of them. The rumored Spreadsheet $ystems merger did not go through, which further depressed the stock price by 20%. The problem was that the company that Spreadsheet $ystems proposed to merge with found another suitor, leaving Spreadsheet $ystems a bit short.

Basically Spreadsheet $ystems is a solid computer software company which needs a shot in the circuits. Its production, distribution, and marketing are good. However, it needs to improve its engineering/design staff to make it. The merger would have given them access to topflight talent.

You're depressed. Your investment in Spreadsheet $ystems has started to lose money after the windfall from the public offering. You could have put your money in a passbook account and done better. You're beginning to think the only way you'll ever get rich and famous is to rob a bank, win the lottery, or write a book on how to make a million dollars with no money down.

You're convinced you should sell your Spreadsheet $ystems stock, but then your friend from the company drops by. He says prospects for the firm never looked better, since it's diversifying into computer hardware. You think if you can't succeed in one area, why not fail in another? The company, he says, is developing a great speech synthesizer that can't fail. Sounds good to you, but if the past is prologue, then it can't do anything but fail.

You wonder whether something less risky might be better suited to your temperament and wallet. Nathaniel has been pushing 10% corporate bond income funds. These are funds which are comprised of debt obligations of corporations. They are safe and liquid. Your return on $239,000 would be almost $24,000. Any profit at all would look good to you now.

But what happens if Spreadsheet $ystems does take off? The numbers seem as helpful as a New York City subway map. Still, you review the current data.

Bank Investment Advisory Newsletter

The economy is on a roll again as the recovery returns. Consumer prices increased only .7% last month, for an annual rate of 8%. The prime rate dropped 1% to 12%. Unemployment declined for the first time in recent memory, to 9%. At the same time the GNP grew at a 6% annualized rate. A host of industries are participating in this turnaround. Car manufacturers, oil companies, and electric utilities reported larger-than-average gains both in unit and dollar volume. Retail sales reported a strong fourth quarter as shoppers flocked to X-mas stores for pre- and post-sales. Even housing demand, pent up for some time, showed some vigor. Housing starts were up 5%.

The index of leading economic indicators was up. Led by stock prices, new orders for consumer goods and materials, and building permits, the index rose 6% versus a year ago. Government spending was also stable, as military spending slowed for the first time in two years. All indicators point to continued improvement for the economy.

SPREADSHEET $YSTEMS
CHAIRMAN'S MESSAGE TO SHAREHOLDERS

Sales climbed to $7.5 million. Steeply rising marketing and administration costs caused the company to report a $1 million loss. Moreover, the outlook is not favorable. Knowledgeable industry observers predict there will be only modest growth in computer software, while competition will intensify.

The management of Spreadsheet $ystems will respond to this challenge by diversifying into computer hardware. We have acquired the rights to Speakeasy ™, a speech synthesizer which reproduces human sound electronically. Our designers have made significant improvements on it. We already have the marketing and distribution apparatus in place. We fully expect first-year sales of the revised Speakeasy ™ unit to exceed $3 million, with a net profit of $500,000. Further increases in software sales also are predicted . . .

DECISION E

The current value of your investment is *$239,400*. Tough luck, your investment is 21% below the average of the experts.

E-5 *Do you go for the small numbers of the 10% corporate bond income fund,* paying $23,940 ($24,000 more than you made previously)? (Turn to page 166.)

or

E-6 *Do you tie your star to Spreadsheet $ystems' Speakeasy ™ speech synthesizer* (that's easy for you to say) and hope that after so many losses the law of averages is on your side? (Turn to page 170.)

After you have made your decision, turn to the next page for the experts' comments.

THE EXPERTS STRATEGIZE: E-5. CORPORATE BOND INCOME FUND

Jonathan Walker (Risk-Averse Expert)—Commentary

Corporate bond funds typically offer advantages over individual corporate bonds because they have diversification and professional management. A professional staff tries to weed out the bonds of weak companies and concentrate on the bonds of strong companies. The yields are typically very good. This bond fund is especially attractive now, given the state of the economy, because if interest rates continue to trend down, the fund could do very well in terms of capital appreciation.

E-6. SPREADSHEET $YSTEMS

Chat Morton (High-Risk Expert)—Commentary

This is not a good investment. Since Spreadsheet $ystems could not compete successfully in an industry that had very low barriers to entry in terms of marketing and designing costs, it now is going into an area that is more competitive and requires greater amounts of capital. The company doesn't have any expertise in this area. You could save yourself a lot of trouble and money by investing in corporate bonds, T bills, or even a 5% passbook account. At least that way you would make some money.

(Continued from page 55)

RESULTS:
D-4. SELL SPREADSHEET $YSTEMS/
ASSET MANAGEMENT ACCOUNT

THE EXPERTS SPEAK
―――――――――――――― Georgina Gold ――――――――――――――

Excellent strategy. You took risks in real estate and Spreadsheet $ystems when you had to and got out when you had made your money there were trouble signs in the company (overcrowded industry, poor profitability, etc.) If I didn't know better, I would think it was investment skill. Your money in the asset management account is in a good holding place, but don't hold it there too long. Stay flexible and try to earn greater returns. So far you have done very well.

As with great comedians and great investors, timing is everything. Knowing when to sell is as important as knowing when to buy. Luck is important, too. You picked the right moment to sell and you were lucky. The Spreadsheet $ystems merger fell through because it looked as though the merger would benefit Spreadsheet $ystems more than the other company. Besides, the other company got a better offer. As a result, Spreadsheet $ystems' stock price dropped 20% to a new low.

At the same time, your asset management account, ever steady and faithful, earned a full 9%, or $26,933. While an asset management account is not the place to keep your money for a long time, it is a good resting place while you study other investment opportunities.

You've been considering bank CDs. They pay a half a percent higher than the asset management account and yet are still fully insured up to $100,000 by the FDIC. A 9 1/2% CD will return over $31,000 on your $326,000 nest egg.

You're about to order CDs when your banker suggests you talk to her husband, Nathaniel the financial advisor. Nathaniel comes over and says, if you want to live a little, why not try options? You wonder how that statement "live a little" should be taken. You would like to live a lot. He suggests options on an index of stocks in the medical technology field. Already that makes you feel better. If the index goes up, you win. You think of the health of the nation and rising medical costs and figure you can't lose. Nathaniel warns you that sometimes new medical technologies, such as the artifical appendix, don't work, and you could lose money.

In any case you feel you have two good choices. Besides, anything is better than Spreadsheet $ystems. You read through the investment advisories, take your financial temperature, and then decide.

Bank Investment Advisory Newsletter

The economy is on a roll again as the recovery returns. Consumer prices increased only .7% last month, for an annual rate of 8%. The prime rate dropped 1% to 12%. Unemployment declined for the first time in recent memory, to 9%. At the same time the GNP grew at a 6% annualized rate. A host of industries are participating in this turnaround. Car manufacturers, oil companies, and electric utilities reported larger-than-average gains both in unit and dollar volume. Retail sales reported a strong fourth quarter as shoppers flocked to X-mas stores for pre- and post-sales. Even housing demand, pent up for some time, showed some vigor. Housing starts were up 5%.

The index of leading economic indicators was up. Led by stock prices, new orders for consumer goods and materials, and building permits, the index rose 6% versus a year ago. Government spending was also stable, as military spending slowed for the first time in two years. All indicators point to continued improvement for the economy.

Option
Opportunities ○ ○ ○ ○ ○ ○ ○ ○ ○ ○ ○ ○ ○ ○ ○ ○

MEDICAL TECHNOLOGY

The Medtech Index is comprised of four companies which manufacture products in the medical technology field. The index has grown an average of 13% in the last three years. Each of the companies is expected to grow significantly in the coming years, especially Heart Pump, Inc., a designer and maker of artificial hearts. Sales were up only slightly from the previous year, but as development of the new technologies progresses, sales should likewise grow. Profits remain low, but this . . .

DECISION E

The current value of your investment is *$326,183.* Congratulations, your investment is 8% above the average of the experts.

E-7 *Do you bank your money in CDs* yielding $30,987 and then sit back, have a few drinks, and worry only about what television program to watch? (Turn to page 174.)

or

E-8 *Do you worry about new advances in medical technology, medical stock prices, and your investment in medical stock index options,* hoping that your companies find a cure for whatever ails people? (Turn to page 177.)

After you have made your decision, turn to the next page for the experts' choices.

THE EXPERTS STRATEGIZE:
E-7. CERTIFICATES OF DEPOSIT

Georgina Gold (Opportunistic Expert) did not take this alternative.

CDs are not a good investment relative to the medical stock index options. While CDs offer plenty of security and a little bit of yield, they wouldn't provide the case of Dom Pérignon you want delivered every Saturday afternoon. The financial opportunity in medical technology options is far greater than in CDs. The CDs do have protection, in that they are insured up to $100,000, but they are unexciting. This is not something you want to spend a year investing in at the age of twenty-nine.

E-8. MEDICAL STOCK INDEX
OPTIONS

Georgina Gold (Opportunistic Expert) took this alternative.

The medical index has grown at 13% a year for the last three years. As the population gets older, there will be a greater demand for artificial hearts and other organs. Sales have been growing as new technologies are developed. It looks like a good bet to invest in this area. Besides, Mother always wanted me to be in medicine.

(Continued from page 60)

RESULTS:
D-5. T BILLS

THE EXPERTS SPEAK
—————————— Jonathan Walker ——————————

Back to the womb. When the real world of investments seemed overly risky, you retreated and bought T bills. It is a smart investor who knows when to consolidate his or her position. Even though American Diversified Industries was in a growth phase, the economy was sputtering along with interest rates and inflation on the rise. American Diversified Industries options may be the right investment, but this is the wrong time. Wait for better economic and market conditions.

A James Bond you're not. Risk to you is trying a new flavor of ice cream—like chocolate or strawberry. However, you're also not sorry. You made a very safe and sound 9.5%, or $13,105, on your $137,948 investment in T bills. Had you chosen options again, you would have lost money. In fact, the other alternative you were considering, options and munis, lost 19% in value.

Still, with the economy and your social life improving, you need to make more money. Nathaniel, your banker's husband and your financial advisor, suggests a tax-free municipal mutual fund. This is a fund composed of debt obligations of non-federal governmental authorities that is not taxable at the federal and sometimes even the state and local level. Because it's diversified, it's safer than individual issues. It's also more liquid—that is, it can easily be sold. Moreover, because it's tax-free, the pre-tax equivalent return is as good as most safe investments and in many cases better. Finally, because bonds in the fund continually mature and new ones are purchased, you can benefit from upturns in interest rates. Previously the fund returned anywhere between 9% and 14% (pre-tax equivalent).

Sounds good, you tell Nathaniel. But what if I really want to improve my social life, like take trips to the Caribbean, ski in Vail, and shop in Bloomingdale's? Then he recommends a combination of futures and money market funds. The money market funds provide safety, while the futures can provide trips, drugs (legal ones only), and the other accoutrements of fine living. The banker's husband suggests a stock index future (the Dow Jones Averages). This means you agree to buy a certain number of shares in this fund for a set price at a specified future date. You also put only a small percentage down (5% to 10%), with the rest guaranteed by you. You can make or lose a fortune with very little down.

Is there life after T bills? The munis fund sounds almost as safe and more profitable than T bills, while the futures can provide comfort for the future. You look at the numbers, smile, and wish.

Bank Investment Advisory Newsletter

The economy is on a roll again as the recovery returns. Consumer prices increased only .7% last month, for an annual rate of 8%. The prime rate dropped 1% to 12%. Unemployment declined for the first time in recent memory, to 9%. At the same time the GNP grew at a 6% annualized rate. A host of industries are participating in this turnaround. Car manufacturers, oil companies, and electric utilities reported larger-than-average gains both in unit and dollar volume. Retail sales reported a strong fourth quarter as shoppers flocked to X-mas stores for pre- and post-sales. Even housing demand, pent up for some time, showed some vigor. Housing starts were up 5%.

The index of leading economic indicators was up. Led by stock prices, new orders for consumer goods and materials, and building permits, the index rose 6% versus a year ago. Government spending was also stable, as military spending slowed for the first time in two years. All indicators point to continued improvement for the economy.

T. KITZINGER'S MARKET OUTLOOK

. . . The Dow Jones Industrials reported moderate gains with trading heavy this year. Led by car, energy, and retail stocks, gainers outnumbered losers 2 to 1. As the economy picked up, most major companies showed substantial increases in fourth-quarter profits.

Excluding older, more traditional industries, e.g., shoes, steel, etc., which are being beaten in the international marketplace, the next year should produce banner results. It is expected that the Dow Jones Averages will climb to . . .

DECISION E

The current value of your investment is $151,053. Tough luck, your investment is 50% below the average of the experts.

E-9 **Do you try a municipal mutual fund with a variable rate** expected to be between 9% and 14%? (Turn to page 181.)

or

E-10 **Do you look into Dow Jones Futures** (with money market funds as backup) and hope that the future is now? (Turn to page 185.)

After you have made your decision, turn to the next page for the experts' comments.

THE EXPERTS STRATEGIZE:
E-9. MUNICIPAL MUTUAL FUNDS

Jonathan Walker (Risk-Averse Expert)—Commentary

Municipal mutual funds offer a very attractive pre-tax equivalent rate of interest. They are diversified. They are professionally managed, so the real disasters may be avoided. For the most part, they offer very good principal protection. That's all they do, but that's plenty.

E-10. DOW JONES FUTURES

Chat Morton (High-Risk Expert)—Commentary

This is an interesting investment since the market recently has rallied strongly. The gainers are outnumbering the losers by a very good percentage. The economy looks good. Inflation, interest rates, and unemployment all are down. Even the traditional industries that are being beaten in the international marketplace could have a good domestic marketplace to sell into over the next year or two. It doesn't look like the bull market is over, which means that this may be a great opportunity to make a lot of money by investing in an index which moves with the market.

(Continued from page 60)

RESULTS:
D-6. OPTIONS/TIME DEPOSITS

THE EXPERTS SPEAK
Georgina Gold

You got thrown for another loss on the option play. Time to move on. Options are too highly speculative for amateurs. American Diversified Industries stock did okay, but it did not go up enough for the options to increase in value. The economy also was not in your favor, since a weak economy makes it more difficult for companies like American Diversified Industries to grow rapidly. Try something else—anything.

Some people never learn. Options are a highly speculative game for the pros, who sometimes win, and for the rich, who can afford not to. Since you don't fit into either one of these categories, you lose. To make money in options you have to be skillful and lucky. It appears you're neither.

Again American Diversified Industries's stock went up, but not enough to make a profit on the option. The 10% gain in revenues was lower than analysts had predicted. Hence the stock gained barely a point on the big board over a year's time. Moreover, after this year's less-than-extraordinary performance most brokerage houses took American Diversified Industries' stock off their buy list.

You figured it was time to sell your options, so you took a 30%, or $41,384, beating. If you hadn't made 11% on the time deposits, your loss would have been far greater than the 19%, or $26,210, you actually suffered. You definitely want to get out of the options market. You contact Nathaniel, your banker's husband, rant and rave about the options he recommended, and then ask for his suggestions. For absolute safety he suggests a 9% government note. With your $112,000; it would return a respectable 10 grand. You blink twice. You could get almost 9% by putting your money into a high-interest savings account. Isn't there anything else you could do? Nathaniel says why not buy drugs and get a high return? You explain you are not trying to finance a car company. He then suggests a combination of a penny stock mutual fund and municipals. He knows a penny stock mutual fund that picks only mining stocks and has had a great record. It has almost broken even over the last five years. For penny stocks that's great. Still, there is always the possibility of striking it rich. Besides, half your money still would be in safe munis.

You're wary of the penny stocks, but not too thrilled at a

9% government note. You have to decide whether you really want yield or safety. Looking at the numbers wouldn't help you decide what your objectives are, but it does provide some comfort: there's always safety in numbers, after all.

Bank Investment Advisory Newsletter

The economy is on a roll again as the recovery returns. Consumer prices increased only .7% last month, for an annual rate of 8%. The prime rate dropped 1% to 12%. Unemployment declined for the first time in recent memory, to 9%. At the same time the GNP grew at a 6% annualized rate. A host of industries are participating in this turnaround. Car manufacturers, oil companies, and electric utilities reported larger-than-average gains both in unit and dollar volume. Retail sales reported a strong fourth quarter as shoppers flocked to X-mas stores for pre- and post-sales. Even housing demand, pent up for some time, showed some vigor. Housing starts were up 5%.

The index of leading economic indicators was up. Led by stock prices, new orders for consumer goods and materials, and building permits, the index rose 6% versus a year ago. Government spending was also stable, as military spending slowed for the first time in two years. All indicators point to continued improvement for the economy.

PENNY STOCK GAZETTE

MINING COMPANIES

. . . Among the mutual funds that are attracting much attention, one which is particularly noteworthy is the Gold Dust Fund. A no-load (i.e., no-fee) penny stock mutual fund composed of new mining companies in the U.S. and Canada, it is professionally managed and shows great promise. After three losing years, the fund is almost breaking even. More important, it has begun to pick companies which are finding gold, uranium, and copper in significant quantities. One company in particular has found large uranium deposits and begun extensive mining operations. The fund now has $10 million to invest, double what it had only a year ago. As the fund has grown, its investments have become more sophisticated . . .

DECISION E

The current value of your investment is *$111,738.* Tough luck, your investment is 63% below the average of the experts.

E-11 *Do you look for long-term guarantees in a no-risk 9% government note,* which will earn you $10,056? (Turn to page 189.)

(Turn to page 189.)

or

E-12 *Do you continue to look for the big strike in a penny stock mutual fund, with munis as backups?* (Turn to page 195.)

(Turn to page 195.)

After you have made your decision, turn to the next page for the experts' comments.

THE EXPERTS STRATEGIZE: E-11. GOVERNMENT NOTES

Jonathan Walker (Risk-Averse Expert)—Commentary

Government notes are like government Treasury bills except they take a little bit longer to mature, about five to ten years (although they can be sold at any time). They're very liquid and extremely safe. They pay a little bit more interest than the government T bills, so your income is slightly higher. A solid, risk-free investment.

E-12. PENNY STOCKS MUTUAL FUND/MUNIS

Chat Morton (High-Risk Expert)—Commentary

This is a very odd combination. Generally you buy the municipals when you're trying to protect income that might be taxed at a very high level. However, with penny stocks as your other main investment, you will probably have only a 20% chance of making a lot of money, so the mix is not really terrific. Still, if the penny stocks do very well, you will be glad you invested in them. If they do poorly, you will be glad you didn't invest your entire savings in them.

(Continued from page 64)

RESULTS: D-7. TIME DEPOSITS

THE EXPERTS SPEAK
Chat Morton

Little risk. Little reward. Your money has grown steadily over the past four years, averaging 12% a year. As interest rates have fallen, you're now looking at a 10% per year growth. If the status quo and steady income is what you want, you found it. Dull. Dull. Dull.

You probably fasten a seat belt when you sit down in a barber's chair to get a haircut. But at least you never fall out, either. In this case you invested in 11% time deposits, which earned a respectable $15,965. At this rate your $160,000 principal will grow a healthy $60,000 in only three years. There is something to be said for safe, stable growth—like being able to pay your bills all the time.

Therefore, you consider keeping your money in time deposits indefinitely. But then Nathaniel, the banker's husband, drops by with a hot stock tip. He knows of a small company in Philadelphia called Washout, Inc., that has invented a new laundry product that will revolutionize the detergent industry. Called CleanUp (pat. pend.), the new product will clean better than anything currently on the market yet will not hurt fabrics and is environmentally safe. You figure what's the big deal since you send your laundry home for Mom to clean. Nathaniel argues that when the product goes national this year, the company's stock will soar. You could invest now while the stock price is still low.

Nathaniel is so enthusiastic about Washout, Inc., that even he is buying stock in the company. That's almost enough reason for you not to, because his last stock recommendation was for a company which made asbestos leisure wear. You ask him how much money he expects the company to make on the new product. He asks, how high is up? That worries you even more. Still, the early investors in a company with a radical new discovery can make a killing by doubling their money the first year. You would need at least seven years to do it in time deposits.

Perhaps you should consider gambling again. You turn on the TV for some investment intelligence. Ponder the issue, and then decide.

Bank Investment Advisory Newsletter

The economy is on a roll again as the recovery returns. Consumer prices increased only .7% last month, for an annual rate of 8%. The prime rate dropped 1% to 12%. Unemployment declined for the first time in recent memory, to 9%. At the same time the GNP grew at a 6% annualized rate. A host of industries are participating in this turnaround. Car manufacturers, oil companies, and electric utilities reported larger-than-average gains both in unit and dollar volume. Retail sales reported a strong fourth quarter as shoppers flocked to X-mas stores for pre- and post-sales. Even housing demand, pent up for some time, showed some vigor. Housing starts were up 5%.

The index of leading economic indicators was up. Led by stock prices, new orders for consumer goods and materials, and building permits, the index rose 6% versus a year ago. Government spending was also stable, as military spending slowed for the first time in two years. All indicators point to continued improvement for the economy.

THE NOW JONES DIGEST WITH JIM TENKAY

> *Out of nowhere, a little Philadelphia, Pennsylvania, chemical company has invented the most exciting new product in years—a new laundry detergent. Using a new bioengineering process,*

> *Washout, Inc., was able to develop a cleaning agent that is both unusually effective and economical to make and use. The product, aptly called CleanUp (pat. pend.), is being rolled out nationally*

> *in only one year. To finance this market rollout, the company has obtained a $50 million line of credit from a local consortium of banks. The company also has been besieged by*

> *offers of financing from venture capitalists. The only question is whether this small, publicly traded company ($10 million in sales last year) can buck the Tides and other detergents of the P & Gs of this world . . .*

DECISION E

The current value of your investment is *$161,104.* Tough luck, your investment is 47% below the average of the experts.

E-13 *Do you continue to watch your money compound in 10% time deposits,* for a gain of $16,110? (Turn to page 199.)

or

E-14 *Do you take a spin with Washout, Inc.,* and hope that the new product cleans up? (Turn to page 202.)

After you have made your decision, turn to the next page for the experts' choices.

THE EXPERTS STRATEGIZE: E-13. TIME DEPOSITS

Jonathan Walker (Risk-Averse Expert) took this alternative.

I took time deposits, because it guaranteed me a respectable rate of return. Moreover, it was a higher rate than I could have earned in the government market. Given the positive attributes of time deposits and my reluctance to give back all the money I have earned over the last four years, time deposits represent an excellent choice.

E-14. WASHOUT, INC.

Jonathan Walker (Risk-Averse Expert) did not take this alternative.

This is a real long shot. Laundry detergents are big business, dominated by giants in the field—P & G, Lever Bros., etc. To believe that a small company can successfully compete with large, well-organized marketing masters based on a new discovery is wishful thinking. The road to success is strewn with the shells of small companies which failed trying to make it big time. I like my money. I'll stick with safe, guaranteed time deposits.

(Continued from page 64)

RESULTS: D-8. DOW JONES INDEX FUND

THE EXPERTS SPEAK
—————— Georgina Gold ——————

Break out the champagne. You took a chance and it worked. Even though the economy was in a holding position at the time you invested in the index, you did well. Since the economy is now improving, there is little reason to change. The Dow Jones has done well in the past and, given the strong and growing economy, should do well in the future.

You tried to play the market with limited risk and it worked. The market is on the rise and the Dow Jones Index Fund you picked did well. It went up 14%, returning $20,319 on your $145,000 investment. With the economy continuing to improve and with blue chips doing especially well, you may have found the key to making money.

You call up your banker's husband and tell him you want to keep your money in the index fund. He tells you he doubts the index fund will continue to return 14%. Besides, he says, there are better ways to make money. You ask him what those ways might be, other than earning a broker's commission. He suggests a new high-flier mutual fund—a can't-lose proposition run by experts. Already you are suspicious. He explains that the mutual fund picks only top computer stocks. Given the explosive growth in the marketplace for home and business computers, how can you possibly lose? You tell him that you had heard that during the initial phases of a new product there are a lot of new entrants in the field, many of whom fail as the industry matures. Couldn't this happen to the computer industry? Of course, Nathaniel responds, but what if you pick the General Motors or the IBM of the industry? The upside potential of the high-flier fund is a lot greater than that of the Dow Jones Index. So is the downside risk, you say.

It's decision time. You look at the numbers and try to guess which is a better investment or which is worse.

Bank Investment Advisory Newsletter

The economy is on a roll again as the recovery returns. Consumer prices increased only .7% last month, for an annual rate of 8%. The prime rate dropped 1% to 12%. Unemployment declined for the first time in recent memory, to 9%. At the same time the GNP grew at a 6% annualized rate. A host of industries are participating in this turnaround. Car manufacturers, oil companies, and electric utilities reported larger-than-average gains both in unit and dollar volume. Retail sales reported a strong fourth quarter as shoppers flocked to X-mas stores for pre- and post-sales. Even housing demand, pent up for some time, showed some vigor. Housing starts were up 5%.

The index of leading economic indicators was up. Led by stock prices, new orders for consumer goods and materials, and building permits, the index rose 6% versus a year ago. Government spending was also stable, as military spending slowed for the first time in two years. All indicators point to continued improvement for the economy.

T. KITZINGER'S MARKET OUTLOOK

. . . The Dow Jones industrials reported moderate gains with trading heavy this year. Led by car, energy, and retail stocks, gainers outnumbered losers 2 to 1. As the economy picked up, most major companies showed substantial increases in fourth-quarter profits. Excluding older, more traditional industries, e.g., shoes, steel, etc., which are being beaten in the international marketplace, the next year should produce banner results. It is expected that the Dow Jones Averages will climb to . . .

INVESTMENT REPORT ON COMPUTER MUTUAL FUNDS

The hottest selling item this year is computers. All models, but especially business personal computers averaging $2,000 and up, are doing extremely well. The

Electronic Industry Association estimates that more than 6.6 million units will be shipped this year. Companies which manufacture computer hardware are experiencing booming sales. To take advantage of this tremendous growth, a new mutual fund has been started which buys only top computer stocks. Last year, stocks in the fund gained a hefty 30%. With the market expecting to triple in the next two years, computer issues should do very well. Current estimates for the fund range in the 20% to 30% range. Future sales . . .

DECISION E

The current value of your investment is *$165,458*. Tough luck, your investment is 45% below the average of the experts.

E-15 **Do you stick with** the success of the past, **the Dow Jones Index Fund,** which yielded 14% last time? (Turn to page 207.)

or

E-16 **Do you try to better your record with a high-flier computer fund,** which could fly high but could also plummet? (Turn to page 211.)

After you have made your decision, turn to the next page for the experts' comments.

THE EXPERTS STRATEGIZE:
E-15. DOW JONES INDEX FUND

Georgina Gold (Opportunistic Expert)—Commentary

An index fund is an inexpensive way to buy into the broad movements of the market. If you wanted to buy each stock individually in the index, you would have to purchase approximately 40 different stocks with additional costs and trouble. The economy is good. The Dow Jones has been going up. You're still in the bull market. It's probably a safe and profitable bet at this point.

E-16. HIGH-FLIER FUND

Chat Morton (High-Risk Expert)—Commentary

You're in the high-growth area of a market, in a fund that has done very well historically. The managers seem to know what they are doing. Last year stocks in the fund gained 30%. The market as a whole is still growing rapidly. There is no reason to believe this trend will not continue. Computers are the hottest thing since chocolate chip cookies. There is more risk in this fund than in the Dow Jones Index, but there also is a real upside potential.

(Continued from page 69)

RESULTS:
D-9. TAX-FREE MUNICIPALS

THE EXPERTS SPEAK
——————— Jonathan Walker ———————

You spent the first three years making your money. Now you'll spend the next three trying to avoid paying taxes on any income it generates. A good strategy? Certainly not a bad one if you stay with the safe, moderate-yielding (10% to 12%) municipals. They are more than competitive with T bills and corporate bonds. Plus everyone loves the idea of not paying taxes. If you don't get greedy and try higher-yielding, more speculative municipals, you're okay.

You finally made it. Your investment strategy is now determined by tax considerations. The most common phrase you use when confronted with an investment opportunity is "It sounds good, but first I'll have to check with my tax attorney." Tax-free municipals are the obvious solution and, to someone in your situation, not a bad choice. With your investment over $350,000 and your 7% munis returning 11.6% (on a pre-tax equivalent basis), you made $40,730. With that kind of income, why work? Why not become a professional investor?

While the 11.6% return is great and relatively safe, you wonder if there are better ways to earn an even greater return, especially since you are a full-fledged member of the nouveau riche, who can afford to take some risks.

You call Leonard, your financial guru, for advice. He still feels munis are a good investment for you, although he recommends a more speculative municipal bond fund if you want a higher yield. He knows a very speculative fund made up of nuclear power bonds (as opposed to less risky highway or housing construction municipal bonds). The nuclear power bonds are dynamite, having returned an average 18% for the last three years. Sounds interesting. Less risky are government securities, or Ginnie Maes, which are fixed-income investments. You buy shares of FHA or VA mortgages, which return interest plus payback on the mortgage. Moreover, they are government-insured. Currently they are paying 12.5%, which would mean over $48,000 for you.

The Ginnie Maes sound great, but the tax-free municipals could pay even more. Besides, you earned your money by gambling. You call up your tax attorney to review the numbers.

Bank Investment Advisory Newsletter

The economy is on a roll again as the recovery returns. Consumer prices increased only .7% last month, for an annual rate of 8%. The prime rate dropped 1% to 12%. Unemployment declined for the first time in recent memory, to 9%. At the same time the GNP grew at a 6% annualized rate. A host of industries are participating in this turnaround. Car manufacturers, oil companies, and electric utilities reported larger-than-average gains both in unit and dollar volume. Retail sales reported a strong fourth quarter as shoppers flocked to X-mas stores for pre- and post-sales. Even housing demand, pent up for some time, showed some vigor. Housing starts were up 5%.

The index of leading economic indicators was up. Led by stock prices, new orders for consumer goods and materials, and building permits, the index rose 6% versus a year ago. Government spending was also stable, as military spending slowed for the first time in two years. All indicators point to continued improvement for the economy.

POWER AUTHORITY BONDS
FREE INFORMATION FROM THEODORE & ASSOC.

Nuclear power has had a bad reputation the last few years. However, investments in power authorities sponsoring nuclear power plants have been very profitable. Because of the riskiness of the investments, individual issues have paid anywhere from 15% to 20% interest— almost double the rate for six-month T bills. One mutual fund, the Sky High Fund, specializing in nuclear issues, has averaged 18% for the past three years. With assets of $3 billion, the Sky High Fund has a diversified portfolio of issues across the country. None of its investments has defaulted. Many of the power plants in its portfolio are near completion and ready for licensing, which is a prerequisite before becoming operational. A $1,000 investment will return . . .

DECISION E

The current value of your investment is *$391,850*. Congratulations, your investment is 30% above the average of the experts.

E-17   ***Do you buy the government securities (Ginnie Maes)*** paying a healthy 12.5%, or $48,981? (Turn to page 215.)

or

E-18   ***Do you put your faith and trust in high-yielding nuclear bonds***, where the sky is the limit? (Turn to page 218.)

After you have made your decision, turn to the next page for the experts' comments.

THE EXPERTS STRATEGIZE: E-17. GINNIE MAES

Jonathan Walker (Risk-Averse Expert)—Commentary

Ginnie Maes are government-guaranteed pools of mortgages, spread out all over the U.S. At a 12% yield plus a return from the normal monthly repayment of principal, this is a terrific product. The yield is far in excess of government Treasury bills or notes and yet is still government-guaranteed. Moreover, there is no real increase in risk. It is one of the mysteries of the market why these investments are traded at a yield so high relative to everything else, given their level of safety and liquidity.

E-18. NUCLEAR POWER AUTHORITY BOND FUND

Chat Morton (High-Risk Expert)—Commentary

On their own, nuclear bonds are risky because of adverse legislation coming out of Congress and the rapidly rising cost of building plants. However, when they come in the form of a large diversified portfolio, particularly the Sky High Fund, some of the risk is diversified away. In this case, the fund is yielding a very high interest rate—about 18%. Most of the power plants are near completion, which is a very big positive. Still, this is a risky investment because of licensing requirements, which often delay or even prevent plants from coming on-line. It is definitely not for the cowardly investor.

(Continued from page 69)

RESULTS:
D-10. OPTIONS/MUNICIPALS

THE EXPERTS SPEAK
Georgina Gold

Options are risky. Options on new companies are even risk-ier. You're lucky you have any money left, since trying to get rich quick is the quickest way to lose all your money. But then again, you gambled successfully on Spreadsheet Systems and did all right. The major difference was luck. The economy is starting to pick up now. Why not look for an investment which is not as risky but still will take advantage of this economic growth.

Money is an opiate: the more you have, the more you want. You picked options and munis because you felt the combination would appreciate more than just munis. Unfortunately, the high-tech company, Light Sat, Inc., never took off. Its commercial satellites proved to be inefficient to produce at present cost. As a result, the company sold few units, with only moderate hope for future sales. While the market regards early losses for high-tech companies as par for the course and even a bit trendy, possible product failure is frowned upon. Hence, the company's stock went down, not up. Your options dropped in value. You broke even only because your munis proved ever-reliable and tax-free.

Once burned, twice cautious. You call up Leonard and tell him anything but options. He suggests real estate. As Will Rogers once said, real estate is a good investment because they ain't making any more of the stuff. Leonard knows of a real estate trust that invests in only high-quality industrial real estate in the Sun Belt. You wonder whether you have ever heard anybody ever describe an investment opportunity as anything but high quality. Still, commercial real estate in the Sun Belt sounds promising. Moreover, this particular trust has yielded 20% per year for the last five years. Of course, if you want a safer alternative there is always a corporate bond income fund paying 10%, or $35,000.

Nobody ever loses money in real estate? You sit down, look at the data, and think of sunshine, cacti, and margaritas as you make your decision.

Bank Investment Advisory Newsletter

The economy is on a roll again as the recovery returns. Consumer prices increased only .7% last month, for an annual rate of 8%. The prime rate dropped 1% to 12%. Unemployment declined for the first time in recent memory, to 9%. At the same time the GNP grew at a 6% annualized rate. A host of industries are participating in this turnaround. Car manufacturers, oil companies, and electric utilities reported larger-than-average gains both in unit and dollar volume. Retail sales reported a strong fourth quarter as shoppers flocked to X-mas stores for pre- and post-sales. Even housing demand, pent up for some time, showed some vigor. Housing starts were up 5%.

The index of leading economic indicators was up. Led by stock prices, new orders for consumer goods and materials, and building permits, the index rose 6% versus a year ago. Government spending was also stable, as military spending slowed for the first time in two years. All indicators point to continued improvement for the economy.

Sun Belt Investment Trust—Prospectus

(Not a formal prospectus. Offering can be made only . . .)

Investment opportunities will be offered in $5,000 units. Payments will be made yearly . . . The Sun Belt Trust invests in commercial office buildings and shopping centers in Florida, Texas, and Arizona. All properties are currently 95% or more occupied. All have long-term (five-year or more) leases remaining. All are located in desirable and growing locations in metropolitan areas.

In the past five years, Sun Belt investments have returned interest and appreciation gains of 20% or more. Future investments . . .

DECISION E

The current value of your investment is *$351,120.* Congratulations, your investment is 16% above the average of the experts.

E-19 **Do you want to invest in Sun Belt land,** the bastion of America's capitalistic system, where you can make or lose your fortune? (Turn to page 222.)

or

E-20 **Do you put your money in a safe, 10% corporate bond income fund,** paying a good $35,112? (Turn to page 227.)

After you have made your decision, turn to the next page for the experts' comments.

THE EXPERTS STRATEGIZE:
E-19. SUN BELT REAL ESTATE

Chat Morton (High-Risk Expert)—Commentary

This looks like an excellent investment opportunity. This particular trust has yielded more than 20% per year for the last five years. All the properties are currently at 95% occupancy. All have lease terms of five years or more. There is no reason to believe, in terms of an income basis, that there will be any change from historical levels. We know the demographics in the Sun Belt have been good. This is almost a guaranteed 20% return. If you're lucky, it could go even higher, to 30% or 40%, as the population and industry continue to shift to the warmer climates. This is one of the outstanding investments to come by my desk in a long time.

E-20. CORPORATE BOND INCOME FUND

Jonathan Walker (Risk-Averse Expert)—Commentary

Corporate bond funds typically offer advantages over buying individual corporate bonds because they have diversification and professional management. A professional staff tries to weed out the bonds of weak companies and concentrate on the bonds of strong companies. The yields are typically very good. This bond fund is especially attractive now, given the state of the economy, because if interest rates continue to trend down, the fund could do very well in terms of capital appreciation.

(Continued from page 73)

RESULTS:
D-11. SPREADSHEET $YSTEMS

THE EXPERTS SPEAK
—————————— **Chat Morton** ——————————

You live and die by the investment sword. As a stock market samurai, you take chances to increase your financial kingdom. For three years the approach has worked. However, very few new companies, with notable exceptions, are able to continuously grow and prosper. Now you have to determine whether Spreadsheet $ystems financial setback is temporary or permanent. The computer software company is diversifying. For most new companies, this is a make-it-or-break-it strategy. Banzai.

You are loyal to a fault. After a spectacular gain when the stock went public, Spreadsheet $ystems has started to lose money. The merger talks fell through. What seemed like a good deal for Spreadsheet $ystems was a great deal, but unfortunately it was not such a great deal for the other company. The other company did merge, but with a separate third company. This left Spreadsheet $ystems holding the bag. As a result, the stock dropped 20%. Your $525,000 investment is now worth $420,000.

All is not lost, says your friend from Spreadsheet $ystems, only your money. Very reassuring. The company has learned the error of its ways and has decided to diversify into computer hardware, the latest craze. Spreadsheet $ystems has developed a speech synthesizer unit that's right on the money. Whose money, you ask. He advises you definitely to keep your shares.

You are skeptical. There are no guarantees in the computer hardware area, any more than in software. Mr. Theodore continues to push muni mutual funds, which are pools of borrowed money from governmental institutions. The return from the municipal fund is tax-free. If you had invested in this fund previously, you would have made almost $70,000 instead of losing $105,000. Municipal mutual funds, he says, are safe and profitable, and besides, he earns a commission on them. This, you realize, is the true logic behind any investment recommendation.

Spreadsheet $ystems' management reports have been anything but enlightening. Still, they are better than nothing. Well, almost better than nothing. You read the report, compare it to the tax-free alternative, and decide.

Bank Investment Advisory Newsletter

The economy is on a roll again as the recovery returns. Consumer prices increased only .7% last month, for an annual rate of 8%. The prime rate dropped 1% to 12%. Unemployment declined for the first time in recent memory, to 9%. At the same time the GNP grew at a 6% annualized rate. A host of industries are participating in this turnaround. Car manufacturers, oil companies, and electric utilities reported larger-than-average gains both in unit and dollar volume. Retail sales reported a strong fourth quarter as shoppers flocked to X-mas stores for pre- and post-sales. Even housing demand, pent up for some time, showed some vigor. Housing starts were up 5%.

The index of leading economic indicators was up. Led by stock prices, new orders for consumer goods and materials, and building permits, the index rose 6% versus a year ago. Government spending was also stable, as military spending slowed for the first time in two years. All indicators point to continued improvement for the economy.

SPREADSHEET $YSTEMS
CHAIRMAN'S MESSAGE TO SHAREHOLDERS

Sales climbed to $7.5 million. Steeply rising marketing and administration costs caused the company to report a $1 million loss. Moreover, the outlook is not favorable. Knowledgeable industry observers predict there will be only modest growth in computer software, while competition will intensify.

The management of Spreadsheet $ystems will respond to this challenge by diversifying into computer hardware. We have acquired the rights to Speakeasy ™, a speech synthesizer which reproduces human sound electronically. Our designers have made significant improvements on it. We already have the marketing and distribution apparatus in place. We fully expect first-year sales of the revised Speakeasy ™ unit to exceed $3 million, with a net profit of $500,000. Further increases in software sales also are predicted . . .

DECISION E

The current value of your investment is $420,000. Congratulations, your investment is 39% above the average of the experts.

E-21 **Do you continue to play the Spreadsheet $ystems investment game,** hoping to win on its computer diversification? (Turn to page 231.)

or

E-22 **Do you invest in safe, 11.5% (after-tax) municipal mutual funds,** knowing that the $48,300 you make will buy a lot of computer hardware and software? (Turn to page 234.)

After you have made your decision, turn to the next page for the experts' choices.

THE EXPERTS STRATEGIZE:
E-21: SPREADSHEET $YSTEMS

Chat Morton (High-Risk Expert) did not take this alternative.

Basically I have made a lot of money up to this point. However, sales are starting to go down. The company has just reported a loss. Growth in the computer software industry is slowing. Competition is intensifying. Spreadsheet $ystems is diversifying into computer hardware, which makes little sense. The handwriting is on the wall. I might as well take my money and move into something more safe, such as municipal bonds. High risk does not mean stupid.

E-22: MUNICIPAL MUTUAL FUNDS

Chat Morton (High-Risk Expert) took this alternative.

The alternative of remaining with Spreadsheet $ystems was completely unappealing. While municipal mutual funds don't offer the spectrum of risk that I would like to incur to develop my money, they do offer me a chance to make back some of what I've lost. This fund provides an opportunity to wait for a new venture to come along that has the proper parameters for me to assume some risk and be rewarded for it.

(Continued from page 73)

RESULTS:
D-12. MUNICIPAL MUTUAL FUND

THE EXPERTS SPEAK
Georgina Gold

Anytime you have a half million dollars to invest, you will make a lot of money even by investing in moderate-yielding instruments. The municipal mutual fund yield was relatively high (13.3%) and relatively safe. The problem with money is the more you have, the more you want. The economy is starting to grow again. Make sure your investments are positioned to grow with it.

Taxes are a burden—only if you have to pay them. The rich generally avoid this burden. You made a wise decision buying a tax-free municipal fund. Your money was safe and yet profitable. You made $70,000 on your $525,000 principal. Spreadsheet $ystems, on the other hand, suffered another setback. The merger attempt failed, which sent the stock price reeling. You feel smug and confident—for at least ten minutes.

After a brief respite, you're anxious to speculate again. You call up Mr. Theodore. He recommends that you keep your money in safe municipal funds. You tell him that's not good enough. Sensing the wanderlust in your eyes and wallet, he recommends penny stocks. You can buy thousands of shares and still keep some of your money in munis. He knows just the penny stocks for you—mining and energy issues in America's last truly wild frontier—California. You ask, isn't California all tapped out? Not for mining and energy issues, he responds.

On the other hand, Mr. Theodore continues, if penny stocks are too much of a crap shoot, you could invest in speculative municipal power authority bond funds. These investments are slightly less risky than penny stocks but still yield high returns. For example, power authority bond funds, which are comprised of nuclear energy issues, are paying up to 18% interest. However, the reason that they pay high rates is that a number of nuclear plants have either met with costly overruns or not come on-line at all. Still, 18% interest makes your eyes light up. As long as they don't glow in the dark, you're okay.

Penny stocks or power authority bonds? You read the reports from the companies and the bank before making a decision.

Bank Investment Advisory Newsletter

The economy is on a roll again as the recovery returns. Consumer prices increased only .7% last month, for an annual rate of 8%. The prime rate dropped 1% to 12%. Unemployment declined for the first time in recent memory, to 9%. At the same time the GNP grew at a 6% annualized rate. A host of industries are participating in this turnaround. Car manufacturers, oil companies, and electric utilities reported larger-than-average gains both in unit and dollar volume. Retail sales reported a strong fourth quarter as shoppers flocked to X-mas stores for pre- and post-sales. Even housing demand, pent up for some time, showed some vigor. Housing starts were up 5%.

The index of leading economic indicators was up. Led by stock prices, new orders for consumer goods and materials, and building permits, the index rose 6% versus a year ago. Government spending was also stable, as military spending slowed for the first time in two years. All indicators point to continued improvement for the economy.

POWER AUTHORITY BONDS

FREE INFORMATION FROM THEODORE & ASSOC.

Nuclear power has had a bad reputation the last few years. However, investments in power authorities sponsoring nuclear power plants have been very profitable. Because of the riskiness of the investments, individual issues have paid anywhere from 15% to 20% interest— almost double the rate for six-month T bills. One mutual fund, the Sky High Fund, specializing in nuclear issues, has averaged 18% for the past three years. With assets of $3 billion, the Sky High Fund has a diversified portfolio of issues across the country. None of their investments has defaulted. Many of the power plants in their portfolio are near completion and ready for licensing, which is a prerequisite before becoming operational. A $1,000 investment will return . . .

PENNY STOCK GAZETTE

MINING COMPANIES

There has been a recent surge in new energy and mining exploration in California. Recent relaxation in conservation laws and new geological testing have suddenly made the land of Hollywood and redwoods a very attractive place to look for gold and energy resources. Exploration and mining north of L.A. and east of San Francisco have just begun and are expected to expand rapidly. Not since the gold rush of '49 and movies of the '30s has California experienced anything like this. Four companies to watch are . . . Each has been capitalized at over $3 million and expects to show profitability in only three years. So far the mining and energy fever has not attracted the major corporations which, therefore, leaves the field wide open. Predictions on finding . . .

DECISION E

The current value of your investment is $594,825.* Congratulations, your investment is 97% above the average of the experts.

E-23 *Do you speculate on penny stocks and munis, in the hope of turning copper into gold?* (Turn to page 238.)

or

E-24 *Do you invest in nuclear energy bonds,* which could light up your future if they don't burn a hole in your wallet? (Turn to page 243.)

After you have made your decision, see the next page for the experts' comments.

THE EXPERTS STRATEGIZE: E-23. PENNY STOCKS MUTUAL FUND/MUNIS

Chat Morton (High-Risk Expert)—Commentary

This is a very odd combination. Generally you buy the municipals when you're trying to protect income that might be taxed at a very high level. However, with penny stocks as your other main investment, you will probably have only a 20% chance of making a lot of money, so the mix is not really terrific. If the penny stocks do very well, you'll be glad you had the municipals. If they do poorly, you will be glad you didn't put your entire savings in them.

E-24. NUCLEAR POWER AUTHORITY BOND FUND

Georgina Gold (Opportunistic Expert)—Commentary

On their own, nuclear bonds are risky because of adverse legislation coming out of Congress and the rapidly rising cost of building plants. However, when they come in the form of a large diversified portfolio, particularly the Sky High Fund, some of the risk is diversified away. In this case, the fund is yielding a very high interest rate, about 18%. Most of the power plants are near completion, which is a very big positive. Still, this is a risky investment because of licensing requirements, which often delay or even prevent plants from becoming operational. It is definitely not for the cowardly investor.

(Continued from page 77)

RESULTS:
D-13. MONEY MARKET FUND

THE EXPERTS SPEAK
Georgina Gold

Since up to this point the economy has given mixed signals, conservative investments made sense. At least you've guaranteed a good but not great return. After making money in the new computer software venture, you have built up your principal slowly but surely. Now that the recovery seems certain, or as certain as anyone can ever be with economic predictions, maybe the time has come to take a risk.

There's nothing wrong with playing it safe—not at 11%, anyway. After your initial Spreadsheet $ystems gamble, you have parlayed your $200,000 into $291,000. The last investment in money market funds yielded $29,000. Not bad, considering your took very little risk in the process.

But do you want to spend the rest of your life earning 11% and going downhill? Current interest rates have dropped a point to 10%. But if not money market funds, then what? Leonard, your financial advisor, cousin, and friend (in that order) calls you. He's got a once-in-a-lifetime opportunity for you, your chance to be famous—your name in lights as a movie producer. Sounds great, you say, but isn't that a bit risky? No, responds Leonard, only if you lose money. There is no way to calculate the exact risk, but millions have been made on the wide screen. (You can't remember the last movie you saw.) The movie deal he proposes is being budgeted at $10 million and has all the ingredients needed for a blockbuster hit: a great director, producer, and star. If things are so great, why do they need your money, you wonder. Still, wouldn't it be great to go to opening night to see your own picture? If this is too risky, Leonard says there are always 10% time deposits.

Despite visions of stardom, you remind yourself that some shooting stars are only visible for a few seconds and some are never seen at all. With almost $300,000 to invest you look at the reports and choose carefully, but not necessarily wisely.

Bank Investment Advisory Newsletter

The economy is on a roll again as the recovery returns. Consumer prices increased only .7% last month, for an annual rate of 8%. The prime rate dropped 1% to 12%. Unemployment declined for the first time in recent memory, to 9%. At the same time the GNP grew at a 6% annualized rate. A host of industries are participating in this turnaround. Car manufacturers, oil companies, and electric utilities reported larger-than-average gains both in unit and dollar volume. Retail sales reported a strong fourth quarter as shoppers flocked to X-mas stores for pre- and post-sales. Even housing demand, pent up for some time, showed some vigor. Housing starts were up 5%.

The index of leading economic indicators was up. Led by stock prices, new orders for consumer goods and materials, and building permits, the index rose 6% versus a year ago. Government spending was also stable, as military spending slowed for the first time in two years. All indicators point to continued improvement for the economy.

MOVIE PROPOSAL—*Only in Lincoln, Nebraska.*

A factory worker who is laid off and must support his family by stealing finds he is much better at crime than he is at anything else and thus must make a difficult choice. Should he move to another city, where there are more affluent victims, or opt not to disrupt his family life . . . This warm and funny story highlights the valiant attempt of one man to provide a better life for his family. The universal themes of love, family, poverty, and crime will strike a responsive chord in the movie-going public. The director has had a string of successes . . . That well-known actor has agreed to star in the lead role . . . The film is being shot on location outside Los Angeles. The picture is budgeted at $10 million and shooting will begin in July.

DECISION E

The current value of your investment is *$290,789.* Tough luck, your investment is 4% below the average of the experts.

E-25 **Do you invest in the glamour of Hollywood?** (Turn to page 247.)

or

E-26 **Do you choose the 10% time deposits,** or $29,079, and buy a video cassette whenever you want to own a piece of Hollywood? (Turn to page 251.)

After you have made your decision, see the next page for the experts' comments.

THE EXPERTS STRATEGIZE:
E-25. HOLLYWOOD/MOVIES

Chat Morton (High-Risk Expert)—Commentary

This is a very tough item to analyze and therefore a tough item to invest in. Most artistic creations require artistic talent to judge. You are making a financial decision. A "warm and funny story" with "universal themes" is probably terrible. The $10 million is only a medium-size budget. This is a very strange enterprise to put your money into; if you're lucky enough to get back 10¢ on the dollar, you've probably had a great success. It's important to separate emotional issues from your investment strategy. Movies are sexy and exciting and related to your dreams. Your investing should be related to reality and your pocketbook. Keeping the two separate will benefit you over the short and long runs.

E-26. TIME DEPOSITS

Jonathan Walker (Risk-Averse Expert)—Commentary

This is a very safe, attractive investment at this point in time. It pays a reasonable 10% with no principal risk. More important, it will give you the time to review other investment proposals, which I think offer better opportunity than the movie idea. Investing in movie proposals is for the super rich, who can afford the glamour and luxury of losing a lot of money in a short period of time.

(Continued from page 77)

RESULTS:
D-14. HIGH-TECH MUTUAL FUND

THE EXPERTS SPEAK
Georgina Gold

Nice try. The High-Tech fund had everything going for it—good track record, good companies, leading-edge technologies, and so forth. Unfortunately, not even the "best" investments always succeed. You took a chance. Luckily it didn't cost you anything. In fact, you even made 3% from your gamble. The safer investments may have returned more, but then again you would not have had the upside potential. Basically it's a question of what level of risk you are comfortable or uncomfortable with.

High-flier funds are great unless they're grounded. Too bad you picked the wrong time to fly. The high-flier fund you invested in had a number of losers. Two computer companies bit the dust, while two others in the fund announced much lower than expected earnings. Despite a strong performance by other companies in the mix, the fund gained only 3%, or $7,859. If you had invested in money market funds, you would have earned 11%, or $28,817. The 8% difference could have bought a lot of happiness.

Time to turn in your high-flier wings and look elsewhere. Leonard, ever-present at investment time, suggests CDs (certificates of deposit). The CDs are insured and offer a return of 11%. After the 3% bath you took in high fliers, you could really clean up in CDs. Doesn't sound bad at all. But things are never that easy. Your friend from Spreadsheet Systems stops by and says it's easy to make 11%, but can you double your money? You stop and think. Your friend says Spreadsheet Systems is diversifying into computer hardware, which should double and even triple sales and earnings. The company has developed a fantastic speech synthesizer unit to spearhead this effort. The company is basing its future on this program. You're speechless. Still, maybe this is a better high-tech alternative. At least you know the company and some of its personnel if it fails.

You review the data, count the money in your wallet, and make a decision.

Bank Investment Advisory Newsletter

The economy is on a roll again as the recovery returns. Consumer prices increased only .7% last month, for an annual rate of 8%. The prime rate dropped 1% to 12%. Unemployment declined for the first time in recent memory, to 9%. At the same time the GNP grew at a 6% annualized rate. A host of industries are participating in this turnaround. Car manufacturers, oil companies, and electric utilities reported larger-than-average gains both in unit and dollar volume. Retail sales reported a strong fourth quarter as shoppers flocked to X-mas stores for pre- and post-sales. Even housing demand, pent up for some time, showed some vigor. Housing starts were up 5%.

The index of leading economic indicators was up. Led by stock prices, new orders for consumer goods and materials, and building permits, the index rose 6% versus a year ago. Government spending was also stable, as military spending slowed for the first time in two years. All indicators point to continued improvement for the economy.

SPREADSHEET $YSTEMS
CHAIRMAN'S MESSAGE TO SHAREHOLDERS

Sales climbed to $7.5 million. Steeply rising marketing and administration costs caused the company to report a $1 million loss. Moreover, the outlook is not favorable. Knowledgeable industry observers predict there will be only modest growth in computer software, while competition will intensify.

The management of Spreadsheet $ystems will respond to this challenge by diversifying into computer hardware. We have acquired the rights to Speakeasy ™, a speech synthesizer which reproduces human sound electronically. Our designers have made significant improvements on it. We already have the marketing and distribution apparatus in place. We fully expect first-year sales of the revised Speakeasy ™ unit to exceed $3 million, with a net profit of $500,000. Further increases in software sales also are predicted . . .

DECISION E

The current value of your investment is *$269,831.* Tough luck, your investment is 11% below the average of the experts.

E-27 **Do you put your money in safe CDs** returning 11%, or $29,681, and sleep safely at night knowing your money is safe? (Turn to page 255.)

or

E-28 **Do you make money the old-fashioned way by gambling on unknown companies like Spreadsheet Systems,** where fortunes are won and lost? (Turn to page 259.)

After you have made your decision, turn to the next page for the experts' comments.

THE EXPERTS STRATEGIZE:
E-27. CERTIFICATES OF DEPOSIT

Jonathan Walker (Risk-Averse Expert)—Commentary
CDs are a solid investment. They are monies which are used by large banks and other financial institutions to help fund their normal lending operations. They provide plenty of security and a low but guaranteed yield. They also are insured up to $100,000 by the federal government. As an investor, you should ask whether you want or need a safe, risk-free investment. The answer to this question will determine whether or not you choose CDs.

E-28. SPREADSHEET $YSTEMS

Chat Morton (High-Risk Expert)—Commentary
This is not a good investment. Since Spreadsheet $ystems could not compete successfully in an industry that had very low barriers to entry in terms of marketing and designing costs, it now is going into an area that is more competitive and requires greater amounts of capital. The company doesn't have any expertise in this area. You could save yourself a lot of trouble and money by investing in corporate bonds, T bills, or even a 5% passbook account. At least that way you would make some money.

(Continued from page 81)

RESULTS:
D-15. CORPORATE BONDS

THE EXPERTS SPEAK
_____ Georgina Gold _____
Having lost money in grain commodities, you were smart not to speculate in gold, since gold is a gambler's game, too. Un-

less you are expert and lucky (and who among us is both), commodities and precious metals are difficult ways to make a killing. Remember the Hunts and their silver debacle. Nonetheless, blue-chip corporate bonds never turn gold. You always make 10% give or take a few hundred dollars. To make money you have to take chances, although the same can be said for losing money, too.

After losing money in commodities, any conservative investment looks good. The corporate bond you invested in returned a safe 10%, or $17,235. At your income level that is nothing to be ashamed of. However, it is also nothing to write home to your broker about.

Leonard, whose firm specializes in the more exotic investments (for example, low-interest Argentinian and Polish bank notes), says speculate. On inquiring what he has in mind, Leonard advises futures, which, he explains, is a commitment to buy or sell stock or any product at an agreed-upon price, the product to be delivered on an agreed-upon date. Rarely, if ever does the investor actually take possession; normally the futures are sold or traded prior to the delivery date. In stock market futures, you make a commitment based upon your best guess as to which way the Dow Jones Averages will go. If you're right, you buy a three-acre estate in the most prestigious part of town. If you're wrong, you move to Sioux City (next to the Corn Palace). Exactly how risky are futures? Leonard admits most people lose money. But he still thinks futures are for you if you're interested in making money.

You ask what happens if you're interested in making more than 10% but not willing to risk your entire $190,000 fortune. Convertible bonds, says Leonard. He explains that convertible bonds are debt issued by a company that can be exchanged or converted into a set number of shares of stock up until the bond matures. It offers a guaranteed return plus some capital appreciation should the stock take off. Leonard recommends American Diversified Industries, a blue-chip company issuing bonds that pay 8% and that are convertible into company stock should that stock increase 10% above its current value. Since the bonds are AA-rated with a "buy" rec-ommendation from all the major brokerage houses, Leonard says you can't lose. "Can't lose," you thought, was a term only gamblers in Las Vegas and Atlantic City used. Still, the con-vertible bonds do sound attractive.

You review the data and decide.

Bank Investment Advisory Newsletter

The economy is on a roll again as the recovery returns. Consumer prices increased only .7% last month, for an annual rate of 8%. The prime rate dropped 1% to 12%. Unemployment declined for the first time in recent memory, to 9%. At the same time the GNP grew at a 6% annualized rate. A host of industries are participating in this turnaround. Car manufacturers, oil companies, and electric utilities reported larger-than-average gains both in unit and dollar volume. Retail sales reported a strong fourth quarter as shoppers flocked to X-mas stores for pre- and post-sales. Even housing de-mand, pent up for some time, showed some vigor. Housing starts were up 5%.

The index of leading economic indicators was up. Led by stock prices, new orders for consumer goods and materials, and building permits, the index rose 6% versus a year ago. Government spend-ing was also stable, as military spending slowed for the first time in two years. All indicators point to continued improvement for the economy.

Street Scene Magazine

"FASHION, FOOD, AND FINANCIAL SERVICES SPELL SUCCESS"

American Diversified Industries is a highly diversified company engaged in fashion, fast foods, and financial services. Its fashion line has been doing reasonably well (8% growth in sales and 6% growth in profits), although it needs to attract a younger, more fashion-oriented crowd to grow in the future. Fast foods is the rising star. The fast food operation opened 50 new theme restaurants last year and plans to open 60 more this year. Its revenues grew 35% and now represent 25% of the American Diversified Industries' total revenue. Financial services has also done well as evidenced by a 25% growth in sales and net income. The company recently sold off its phone equipment line and is reportedly looking for acquisitions to spend its large cash assets on. The P/E ratio is only 8, a remarkably low figure given the past success and growth of American Diversified Industries.

T. KITZINGER'S MARKET OUTLOOK

. . . The Dow Jones Industrials reported moderate gains with trading heavy this year. Led by car, energy, and retail stocks, gainers outnumbered losers 2 to 1. As the economy picked up, most major companies showed substantial increases in fourth-quarter profits.

Except for older, more traditional industries, e.g., shoes, steel, etc., which are being beaten in the international marketplace, the next year should produce banner results. It is expected that the Dow Jones Averages will climb to . . .

DECISION E

The current value of your investment is $189,585. Tough luck, your investment is 38% below the average of the experts.

E-29 **Do you buy the convertible bonds** with the guaranteed 8% return plus bond appreciation? (Turn to page 262.)

or

E-30 **Do you try to guess the future and win a fortune on Dow Jones Futures?** (Turn to page 267.)

After you have made your decision, see the next page for the experts' comments.

THE EXPERTS STRATEGIZE:
E-29. CONVERTIBLE DEBENTURES

Jonathan Walker (Risk-Averse Expert)—Commentary

Convertible debentures have two main advantages: a guaranteed yield, which makes them like a bond, but also upside potential should the stock rally. American Diversified Industries is a solid company. Revenues and profits are increasing at a moderate rate. The company has large cash assets. The bond yield will protect you on the downside, while there is an upside possibility should the stock price rise.

E-30. DOW JONES FUTURES

Chat Morton (High-Risk Expert)—Commentary

This is an interesting investment since the market recently has rallied strongly. The gainers are outnumbering the losers by a very good percentage. The economy looks good. Inflation, interest rates, and unemployment all are down. Even the traditional industries that are being beaten in the international marketplace could have a good domestic marketplace to sell into over the next year or two. It doesn't look like the bull market is over. If it isn't, you have a great opportunity to make a lot of money by investing in an index which moves with the market.

(Continued from page 81)

RESULTS:
D-16. GOLD FUTURES/CORPORATE BONDS

THE EXPERTS SPEAK
Georgina Gold

Sadder but wiser. Speculating is a tough way to make a living, especially when you do it with your own money. Gold has been a roller-coaster investment with extreme highs and lows, most of which are beyond the control of the investor. Other investments are more predictable but also less rewarding. Diamonds, as opposed to gold, are tightly controlled by a cartel, which should provide greater price protection against fickle governments and investment publics.

In theory gold is the ultimate hedge against bad news. Amidst war, violence, and international terrorism, you figured that the only place that the price of gold could go was up. Since interest rates were declining, gold was a particularly attractive investment. Unfortunately, bad news forced foreign governments to sell off their gold reserves to finance their war extravaganzas. As a result, the supply of gold increased, the price declined, and you lost $50,000. So much for gold.

While Leonard realizes that gold may not have been right for you (that's an understatement), diamonds are a person's best friend. You wonder. Leonard explains that diamonds are controlled by a cartel which regulates the world's supply. If you invest wisely in diamonds, your investment can only appreciate. Your eyes begin to sparkle. Then you think of the oil cartel and its fiascos and begin to worry. Can't you also lose on diamonds? Of course, says Leonard, but you have to take risks to make money. If you want to be completely safe, you could always invest in 10% certificates of deposits. CDs are comforting—but diamonds are appealing.

You look at the data and reports before you try to determine your financial fate.

Bank Investment Advisory Newsletter

The economy is on a roll again as the recovery returns. Consumer prices increased only .7% last month, for an annual rate of 8%. The prime rate dropped 1% to 12%. Unemployment declined for the first time in recent memory, to 9%. At the same time the GNP grew at a 6% annualized rate. A host of industries are participating in this turnaround. Car manufacturers, oil companies, and electric utilities reported larger-than-average gains both in unit and dollar volume. Retail sales reported a strong fourth quarter as shoppers flocked to X-mas stores for pre- and post-sales. Even housing demand, pent up for some time, showed some vigor. Housing starts were up 5%.

The index of leading economic indicators was up. Led by stock prices, new orders for consumer goods and materials, and building permits, the index rose 6% versus a year ago. Government spending was also stable, as military spending slowed for the first time in two years. All indicators point to continued improvement for the economy.

PRECIOUS METTLE □ □□ □
An investment analysis□ □

DIAMONDS—INVESTMENT OUTLOOK

Diamond prices have started to climb. After a year of relative price stability, diamonds are in vogue again. Latest designs out of Paris, Rome, and New York feature lots of jewelry and glitter, and the more the better. The South African cartel has curtailed production in the face of rising demand in an effort to boost prices. Other world producers seem to be cooperating, even the Russians. The only threat to this seeming unity could arise from the need to raise capital by . . . As investments, diamond mining companies are preferred to raw stones. Industrial grade diamonds are in great demand, as are . . .

DECISION E

The current value of your investment is $122,350. Tough luck, your investment is 60% below the average of the experts.

E-31 *Do you figure that a guaranteed 10% CD, or $12,235, is worth far more than diamonds* in the sky? (Turn to page 271.)

or

E-32 *Do you figure diamonds are forever?* (Turn to page 274.)

After you have made your decision, see the next page for the experts' comments.

THE EXPERTS STRATEGIZE: E-31. CERTIFICATES OF DEPOSIT

Jonathan Walker (Risk-Averse Expert)—Commentary

CDs are a solid investment. They are monies which are used by large banks and other financial institutions to help fund their normal lending operations. They provide plenty of security and a low but guaranteed yield. They also are insured up to $100,000 by the federal government. As an investor, you should ask whether you want or need a safe, risk-free investment. The answer to this question will determine whether or not you choose CDs.

E-32. DIAMONDS

Chat Morton (High-Risk Expert)—Commentary

The value of diamonds historically has grown at an annual rate that would be in excess of anything else you could invest in. Currently there is a great rush into investing into material objects as opposed to financial assets. The problem is you don't really know too much about diamonds and can't control the factors that affect their price. You lack the ability to price diamonds accurately. Over the long haul it is probably a good investment due to the DeBeers cartel. In the short term you could easily have a dip in the market.

(Continued from page 85)

RESULTS: E-1. CONVERTIBLE BONDS

THE EXPERTS SPEAK
Jonathan Walker

See what happens when you take a chance on a good company? You make money: 20%. The lesson is clear. If you buy value or quality, you can't go too far wrong. Millions of dollars have been made investing in IBM, Xerox, and General Motors. The economy is doing well again, which helps the diverse product line of Current Technologies. The company looks solid. Think carefully before investing in another "opportunity."

So you decided to hold the convertible debentures. You made some money from interest, but you did even better as the stock took off. Your investment increased a total of 20%, or nearly $45,000. Nathaniel was right about the potential of Current Technologies.

The future also looks bright. The multinational, multiproduct, multiconglomerate, multieverything Current Technologies reports record earnings and record growth. Nathaniel recommends keeping the debentures. While the numbers look excellent, you are uncertain—given that he would have to be right twice in a row. Do wonders never cease?

You wonder what the alternative is. Nathaniel replies 9% time deposits. He says they're safe, reliable, and boring. Wouldn't you rather see the bright lights of Current Technologies in your future? You say yes, as long as no one pulls the plug. While time deposits will never fail, they are not shining investments in today's bull market economy.

You look at the data, turn on and off and on the lights by Current Technologies and then decide.

Bank Investment Advisory Newsletter

The economy continues to flex its muscle. The GNP grew 8% for the year. The index of leading economic indicators also gave the current administration something to cheer about, as the index grew a full 1%, led by the growth in the formation of new businesses and a dip in unemployment claims. Retail sales climbed above the monthly $100 billion level as Sears, J. C. Penney, and K Mart reported banner sales for the year. Inflation fell to 7%, while unemployment remained at 9%. New car sales are above the 10 million annual rate, while steel companies are showing some strength in cutting losses and fighting foreign competition. Corporate profits as a whole grew 13%, while the Dow Jones Industrial Averages set new records. At the same time the prime rate dropped another percent to 11% as rates across the board fell.

Government spending is under control, although conservatives and hawks condemn the recent lids on military spending, while liberals and social welfare advocates call the administration's reductions in the social welfare area unconscionable. Still, taxpayers who are paying less and consumers who are spending more are highly supportive . . .

Street Scene Magazine

"STRATEGY IS THE KEY TO SUCCESS FOR CURRENT TECHNOLOGIES"

. . . Sales and profits continue to increase in the high double-digit range. Abetted by a large order from Sears and Penney, the consumer electronics division is booming. Industrial products, tried-and-true, have found their way into numerous space and military hardware. Current Technologies management forecasts growth in revenues and profits in the 20% ballpark. There does not seem to be any reason to doubt that. The company is strategically well positioned against foreign and domestic competitors . . .

DECISION F

The current value of your investment is $268,536. Tough luck, your investment is 19% below the average of the experts.

F-1 **Do you tie your future to** the rising star of **Current Technologies?** (Turn to page 279.)

or

F-2 **Do you go back to safe, reliable 9% time deposits** yielding $24,168, so at least you'll know where your money is at all times? (Turn to page 280.)

After you have made your decision, see the next page for the experts' comments.

THE EXPERTS STRATEGIZE:
F-1. CONVERTIBLE DEBENTURES

Chat Morton (High-Risk Expert)—Commentary

The key rule of investing is to cut your losses short and let your profits run wild. There is no reason to believe that the stock of Current Technologies is going to go down. You have been successful with the company in the past, and the company has been doing very well in the marketplace. Every division of the company is profitable. This seems to be a terrifically well-managed company. I would keep the convertible debentures.

F-2. TIME DEPOSITS

Jonathan Walker (Risk-Averse Expert)—Commentary

Time deposits are among the safest investments you can make. They are typically for very short periods of time, ranging from one week to several years. You get a fixed return, and your investment is guaranteed up to $100,000 by the FDIC. The one unattractive feature of time deposits is that they are not marketable, meaning you must pay a penalty if you withdraw your money before they mature. But in general they are good, sound investments.

(Continued from page 85)

RESULTS:
E-2. SELL DEBENTURES/BUY CORPORATE NOTE

THE EXPERTS SPEAK
Chat Morton

You know where your money is at all times. That is the major advantage and the primary disadvantage of corporate notes. You know you're not going to lose your money, but you also know you're not going to be a millionaire overnight. The economy is showing signs of vitality. Interest rates are down, while the GNP is up. Maybe now is the time to consider investing in America's growth. That may be the best way to increase your principal, too.

You went against your broker's advice, so instead of making $45,000 you made only $25,000. Oh well, brokers are not always wrong—just most of the time. You just played the law of averages betting Nathaniel, your banker's husband, would be wrong. He wasn't. Nathaniel drops by. It's easier to gloat in person than by phone. However, he says all is not lost. You still have a chance to play the market and make some real money. How? Stock indices, he says.

Like you, stock index funds are conservative. You buy a fund made up of the Standard and Poor's 500 stocks. When the index goes up, the value of your investment likewise increases. Simple. You take advantage of the upside potential of the market without the horrendous risk of investing in a single stock. Sounds good, you think, unless the market goes down. Now is not the time to be skittish, advises Nathaniel. Ride the bull market. But if you want to play it real safe you could always invest in lowly 9% corporate bonds, returning $22,000. You already made that mistake once.

It's easy to be confident and risky with someone else's money. You want to look at the numbers first, look at the risks, and then make a decision.

Bank Investment Advisory Newsletter

The economy continues to flex its muscle. The GNP grew 8% for the year. The index of leading economic indicators also gave the current administration something to cheer about, as the index grew a full 1%, led by the growth in the formation of new businesses and a dip in unemployment claims. Retail sales climbed above the monthly $100 billion level as Sears, J. C. Penney, and K Mart reported banner sales for the year. Inflation fell to 7%, while unemployment remained at 9%. New car sales are above the 10 million annual rate, while steel companies are showing some strength in cutting losses and fighting foreign competition. Corporate profits as a whole grew 13%, while the Dow Jones Industrial Averages set new records. At the same time the prime rate dropped another percent to 11% as rates across the board fell.

Government spending is under control, although conservatives and hawks condemn the recent lids on military spending, while liberals and social welfare advocates call the administration's reductions in the social welfare area unconscionable. Still, taxpayers who are paying less and consumers who are spending more are highly supportive . . . .

T. KITZINGER'S MARKET OUTLOOK

The market has never been stronger. Trading is heavy with 100-million-share days no longer uncommon. The economy seems for the moment to be under control. Inflation is in check while interest rates have declined. The Dow Jones Averages have rallied in the past three months. The Standard and Poor's 500 gained 10 points over the last quarter. A composite index shows losers are now a small . . . For the next six to nine months, economists at the major brokerage houses are predicting continued strong performance with some big winners and very few losers. Institutional buying continues to be heavy, especially in blue-chip and energy issues. Attractive stocks to watch are . . .

DECISION F

The current value of your investment is *$248,396*. Tough luck, your investment is 25% below the average of the experts.

F-3 ***Do you invest your money in safe, 9% corporate bonds,*** for a $22,356 gain? (Turn to page 279.)

or

F-4 ***Do you hope the bulls stampede the market and send the S & P index soaring?*** (Turn to page 280.)

After you have made your decision, see the next page for the experts' comments.

THE EXPERTS STRATEGIZE:
F-3. CORPORATE BONDS

Jonathan Walker (Risk-Averse Expert)—Commentary

Corporate bonds typically are very safe. They are debt with a senior claim on a company's assets if the company develops any problems. The 9% interest rate is good. The only risk is if interest rates go up sharply, then the price of the bonds will drop. It is possible to reduce this risk by buying shorter term bonds.

The economy seems to favor an investment of this type. Inflation is falling, which should help interest rates. As a result, in the near term there should be little principal risk. In addition, the bonds provide a decent return from interest.

F-4. STANDARD AND POOR'S
INDEX FUND

Georgina Gold (Opportunistic Expert)—Commentary

An index fund is an inexpensive way to buy into the broad movements of the market. If you wanted to buy each stock individually in the index, you would have to purchase approximately 500 different stocks. By buying a share in the fund, you avoid these additional costs and trouble.

This looks like it would be an excellent investment. The economy is good. Government spending is under control. The stock market has never been stronger. Institutional buying is very heavy, with prices going up. All the economic statistics are pointing to higher prices. The Standard and Poor's Index, by giving you access to 500 stocks, will make sure that you participate in an upward move in the market.

(Continued from page 89)

RESULTS:
E-3. T BILLS

THE EXPERTS SPEAK
Georgina Gold

Anything the government issues is safe, but not very profitable. You made 9%, which is better than the alternative, penny stocks. Still, with a growing economy there are opportunities to make money which you should not ignore. A healthy marketplace means there are companies out there making money.

Your true colors are showing—dull conservative. Despite the chance to speculate in penny stocks, you saved your pennies and invested in government securities. How dull. You made only 9%, or $20,503. But how wise. Had you invested in risky penny stocks, you would have made nothing. You call up your broker to gloat. Then you ask what he can recommend so that you can make more money yet not be taken to the cleaners—or lose your shirt altogether.

Nathaniel suggests Dow Jones Futures, which are commitments to buy stock at an agreed-upon price for delivery at an agreed-upon date. Rarely if ever does the investor actually take possession; normally the futures are traded or sold prior to the delivery date. If you think you know which way the market is going, you make money. It's that simple. Of course, if the market goes the other way, you lose. That's simple too. Since you can buy futures by putting down a small percent, you can make or lose big bucks. However, it's important to remember that you have to be able to cover your losses. What losses? you say.

You ask, what if you don't want to take the risk? Then, he responds, you invest in safe, 8.5% CDs. But he also reminds you that you said you wanted to do better. Here's your chance.

Undecided, you sit, think, read, and then decide.

Bank Investment Advisory Newsletter

The economy continues to flex its muscle. The GNP grew 8% for the year. The index of leading economic indicators also gave the current administration something to cheer about, as the index grew a full 1%, led by the growth in the formation of new businesses and a dip in unemployment claims. Retail sales climbed above the monthly $100 billion level as Sears, J. C. Penney, and K Mart reported banner sales for the year. Inflation fell to 7%, while unemployment remained at 9%. New car sales are above the 10 million annual rate, while steel companies are showing some strength in cutting losses and fighting foreign competition. Corporate profits as a whole grew 13%, while the Dow Jones Industrial Averages set new records. At the same time the prime rate dropped another percent to 11% as rates across the board fell.

Government spending is under control, although conservatives and hawks condemn the recent lids on military spending, while liberals and social welfare advocates call the administration's reductions in the social welfare area unconscionable. Still, taxpayers who are paying less and consumers who are spending more are highly supportive . . .

T. KITZINGER'S
MARKET OUTLOOK

The market has never been stronger. Trading is heavy with 100-million-share days no longer uncommon. The economy seems for the moment to be under control. Inflation is in check while interest rates have declined. The Dow Jones Averages have rallied in the past three months. The Standard and Poor's 500 gained 10 points over the last quarter. A composite index shows losers are now a small . . . For the next six to nine months, economists at the major brokerage houses are predicting continued strong performance with some big winners and very few losers. Institutional buying continues to be heavy, especially in blue-chip and energy issues. Attractive stocks to watch are . . .

DECISION F

The current value of your investment is $248,316. Tough luck, your investment is 25% below the average of the experts.

F-5 **Do you** believe there is no quick-and-easy way to get rich and so **invest in 8.5% CDs**, returning $21,107? (Turn to page 279.)

or

F-6 **Do you believe that gambling on futures** could be your shortcut to happiness? (Turn to page 280.)

After you have made your decision, see the next page for the experts' comments.

THE EXPERTS STRATEGIZE:
F-5. CERTIFICATES OF DEPOSIT

Jonathan Walker (Risk-Averse Expert)—Commentary

CDs are a solid investment. They are monies which are used by large banks and other financial institutions to help fund their normal lending operations. They provide plenty of security and a low but guaranteed yield. They also are insured up to $100,000 by the federal government. As an investor, you should ask whether you want or need a safe, risk-free investment. The answer to this question will determine whether or not you choose CDs.

F-6. DOW JONES FUTURES

Georgina Gold (Opportunistic Expert)—Commentary

Futures are an extremely risky investment. They are even riskier than options, since you are never exactly sure what your total losses might be. If the index goes up, the value of your futures will go up accordingly. If the index goes down, you could take a very large loss.

At this point it looks like Dow Jones Futures might be a safe bet, but you are going to need a very strong stomach. The market has never been stronger. The economy is extremely robust, and all the economic indices are doing better. Institutions are realizing this and have been buying stocks very heavily. It's a good bet stock prices will continue to go up, and therefore futures could be very profitable.

(Continued from page 89)

RESULTS:
E-4. PENNY MINING STOCKS/MUNIS

THE EXPERTS SPEAK
―――――――――― **Jonathan Walker** ――――――――――

After choosing relatively safe investments in time deposits, corporate bonds, mutual funds, and real estate, you decided to go big time and invest in risky penny stocks. Penny stocks are a major gamble—clear and simple. Penny stock companies have trouble raising money other ways and fail a lot more often then they succeed. Moreover, the success rate of mining companies is low. Therefore, a penny stock mining company is a double whammy.

Penny stocks are the last frontier of American capitalism, hope, and greed, but not necessarily in that order. If hope springs eternal, you may have a long wait. You invested in four penny stock mining companies. In fact, you almost own two of them. If any of them had found anything, you would have made a fortune. Unfortunately, none of them did, and you took a beating. Luckily, you had munis as a safety value. After computing in the losses from the penny stocks and gains from the munis, your total investment remained the same. How does it feel to have gained nothing in the last year?

Still, where there is greed, there is hope. The penny stocks may turn around after all, advises Nathaniel. But you are wary. What happens if they don't? Then you should buy a penny stock mutual fund, he suggests. If only a few of the issues do well, you could do very well. Again he recommends a fund in the mining area. If you are tired of penny stocks, though, there are always safe, 8.2% T bills, which would pay almost $19,000.

Greed, hope, and fortune—versus safety, security, and the government. A tough choice. Of course you look at the numbers, but your heart makes the decision.

Bank Investment Advisory Newsletter

The economy continues to flex its muscle. The GNP grew 8% for the year. The index of leading economic indicators also gave the current administration something to cheer about, as the index grew a full 1%, led by the growth in the formation of new businesses and a dip in unemployment claims. Retail sales climbed above the monthly $100 billion level as Sears, J. C. Penney, and K Mart reported banner sales for the year. Inflation fell to 7%, while unemployment remained at 9%. New car sales are above the 10 million annual rate, while steel companies are showing some strength in cutting losses and fighting foreign competition. Corporate profits as a whole grew 13%, while the Dow Jones Industrial Averages set new records. At the same time the prime rate dropped another percent to 11% as rates across the board fell.

Government spending is under control, although conservatives and hawks condemn the recent lids on military spending, while liberals and social welfare advocates call the administration's reductions in the social welfare area unconscionable. Still, taxpayers who are paying less and consumers who are spending more are highly supportive . . .

PENNY STOCK GAZETTE

MINING MUTUAL FUNDS

Penny stock mining funds are a dime a dozen. Most hope the law of averages will work in the investors' favor. That's like going to Florida and praying for snow. But there is one new fund that looks stronger than most. The U-Mine Mutual Fund was started by a geologist for wealthy members of his family, who are now even wealthier. The fund has invested in sixteen companies, two of which have succeeded in making valuable finds. The fund is now being sold to the public on the penny stock exchange. It currently has $10 million in assets and last year had a remarkable return of 40%. While there are no guarantees that this will be repeated . . .

DECISION F

The current value of your investment is $227,813. Tough luck, your investment is 31% below the average of the experts.

F-7 **Do you put your faith and fortune in a penny stock mutual fund,** which could make or break your financial future? (Turn to page 279.)

or

F-8 **Do you** not tempt the hands of fate and **buy U.S. Treasury bills,** which pay a guaranteed 8.2%, or $18,681? (Turn to page 280.)

After you have made your decision, see the next page for the experts' comments.

THE EXPERTS STRATEGIZE: F-7. PENNY MINING STOCKS MUTUAL FUND

Chat Morton (High-Risk Expert)—Commentary

Penny stock investments are in general very risky. The underlying penny stock companies are by definition not financially sound. Mining stocks add an additional element of risk. They are dependent not only on their ability to find valuable metal but also on the market value or price of that metal. Although this fund is diversified, it is still a risky investment. Only two out of sixteen have made successful finds. That means the other fourteen are in precarious financial shape, without any real asset base. Although the fund gained 40% last year, this is a very risky investment and should be avoided at all costs.

F-8. T BILLS

Jonathan Walker (Risk-Averse Expert)—Commentary

T bills are absolutely the safest investment to put your money into. There is no risk on the principal. Your interest will be paid by the U.S. government. This is the place to put money when you don't really know what you want to do with it, yet you want to make sure you have it when you want it. Money can be withdrawn from T bills at any time. The markets are extremely liquid.

(Continued from page 93)

RESULTS:
E-5. CORPORATE BOND INCOME FUND

THE EXPERTS SPEAK
Chat Morton

After making money speculating on real estate and Spreadsheet $ystems, you lost a few dollars, which drove you to a safe corporate bond fund. He or she who lives by speculation dies by it, but oh what a short, happy life. Your 10% return in a growing economy is nothing short of disgraceful. There is plenty of opportunity out there. Live free and die young if you have to.

You decided to pull the plug on your Spreadsheet $ystems investment. You had serious doubts about a four-year-old company that has had two years of flat or declining earnings. The thrill is gone. Well, you did the right thing. Spreadsheet $ystems' attempt to diversify failed. Spreadsheet $ystems learned that computer hardware is no easier to sell than computer software. So instead of suffering a loss, your decision to sell your stock and buy a 10% corporate bond income fund returned almost $24,000.

You're happy. At least you made money. But is $24,000 enough? What if you wanted to hire a full-time chauffeur or valet? You could hardly do that on the pittance you're currently receiving. Maybe you should become more adventuresome. You've seen advertisements in the paper for gold. You remember Humphrey Bogart and John Huston lusting for gold in *Treasure of Sierra Madre*. Men and women have killed for gold. Maybe you should put your funds there.

You call up Leonard, who recommends buying shares in gold mining companies in Canada. The companies are a little less volatile than the bullion market but still rise and fall with world gold prices. Already you're salivating. Still, Leonard urges caution since gold is highly speculative. The corporate bond fund will return 10%, or $26,000, which will look like a fortune if gold loses its glamour. You have gold fever, but you still review the data and numbers.

Bank Investment Advisory Newsletter

The economy continues to flex its muscle. The GNP grew 8% for the year. The index of leading economic indicators also gave the current administration something to cheer about, as the index grew a full 1%, led by the growth in the formation of new businesses and a dip in unemployment claims. Retail sales climbed above the monthly $100 billion level as Sears, J. C. Penney, and K Mart reported banner sales for the year. Inflation fell to 7%, while unemployment remained at 9%. New car sales are above the 10 million annual rate, while steel companies are showing some strength in cutting losses and fighting foreign competition. Corporate profits as a whole grew 13%, while the Dow Jones Industrial Averages set new records. At the same time the prime rate dropped another percent to 11% as rates across the board fell.

Government spending is under control, although conservatives and hawks condemn the recent lids on military spending, while liberals and social welfare advocates call the administration's reductions in the social welfare area unconscionable. Still, taxpayers who are paying less and consumers who are spending more are highly supportive . . .

PRECIOUS METTLE ☐ ☐ ☐
An investment analysis ☐ ☐

THE OUTLOOK FOR GOLD

The low price of gold continues to confound analysts. Gold was expected to rise after apparently bottoming out in the early '80s. Given the world instability and the need for financial security, predictions were made that gold would increase a minimum of 30% in value during the past year. This has not happened. In addition, the supply of gold has not expanded as much as was forecast. The effect of the bank debt abroad is uncertain. Analysts are divided on the future of gold and its value as an investment . . .

DECISION F

The current value of your investment is *$263,340*. Tough luck, your investment is 20% below the average of the experts.

F-9 ***Do you invest in conservative corporate bond income funds*** paying a fixed 10% yield, or $26,334? (Turn to page 279.)

or

F-10 ***Do you hope there will be a new rush for gold,*** sending shares through the roof? (Turn to page 280.)

After you have made your decision, see the next page for the experts' comments.

THE EXPERTS STRATEGIZE: F-9. CORPORATE BOND INCOME FUND

Jonathan Walker (Risk-Averse Expert)—Commentary

This fund continues to be a good, solid investment. Since it is a portfolio of different corporate issues of varying maturities, it offers a competitive yield and yet still is very safe. It is professionally managed, which also adds to its safety and yield. This is an excellent investment if income and safety are your primary investment criteria.

F-10. GOLD SHARES

Georgina Gold (Opportunistic Expert)—Commentary

The critical factor to consider with this investment is the future price of gold. If the price goes up, you will make a lot of money on gold shares. If the price goes down, you will lose a lot. In general this is a very risky investment, because it is difficult if not impossible to determine the future price of gold. The reason for this is that there are a lot of factors beyond your control or ability to predict, such as world politics, world disasters, and the South African government and its willingness to expand or contract the supply of gold. Since you are buying shares in companies, you also are betting these companies will mine efficiently and find new sources of gold—an additional risk. I would be very cautious about an investment of this type.

(Continued from page 93)

RESULTS:
E-6. SPREADSHEET $YSTEMS

THE EXPERTS SPEAK
Chat Morton

Your faith in Spreadsheet $ystems is admirable and blind. You ignored all the telltale signs of a troubled company— slumping sales, loss of profitability, an overcrowded marketplace, lack of clear direction, and so forth. Only politicians and priests are more confused and more hopeful under these circumstances. A good investor knows when it is time to quit. There is something to be said for making money, even if it's only 9.5%.

The attempt of Spreadsheet $ystems to diversify into computer hardware was short-circuited. The computer hardware field, like the software field, is crowded. Entry costs are relatively low, but so are chances of success. Speech synthesizer units from a company whose financial programs are doing only fair didn't exactly instill confidence. As a result, the hardware foray was not successful and your Spreadsheet $ystems shares declined another 25%, or nearly $60,000, in value. Company prospects do not look good.

Your friend from the company says the decline is only temporary. (You wonder if it's only temporary because the company is going out of business.) He says keep your shares because the company may be a candidate for an acquisition, which should drive the price of the shares up. If Spreadsheet $ystems is not acquired, then you had better hope for a resurgence in the software market. You are not optimistic.

Leonard, your cousin and part-time financial mentor, calls to remind you that you could always invest in a safe, 9.5% corporate bond income fund should your dementia be cured. A corporate bond income fund, he explains, is a diversified group of corporate bonds or debt issues offering the investor a relatively high but safe yield. To keep your money in Spreadsheet $ystems is like betting at the track—you can't really win. But, you think, at least you'd have fun trying.

You need time to think and ponder your future. After ten minutes of reviewing the data, you decide.

Bank Investment Advisory Newsletter

The economy continues to flex its muscle. The GNP grew 8% for the year. The index of leading economic indicators also gave the current administration something to cheer about, as the index grew a full 1%, led by the growth in the formation of new businesses and a dip in unemployment claims. Retail sales climbed above the monthly $100 billion level as Sears, J. C. Penney, and K Mart reported banner sales for the year. Inflation fell to 7%, while unemployment remained at 9%. New car sales are above the 10 million annual rate, while steel companies are showing some strength in cutting losses and fighting foreign competition. Corporate profits as a whole grew 13%, while the Dow Jones Industrial Averages set new records. At the same time the prime rate dropped another percent to 11% as rates across the board fell.

Government spending is under control, although conservatives and hawks condemn the recent lids on military spending, while liberals and social welfare advocates call the administration's reductions in the social welfare area unconscionable. Still, taxpayers who are paying less and consumers who are spending more are highly supportive . . .

SPREADSHEET $YSTEMS
CHAIRMAN'S MESSAGE TO SHAREHOLDERS

Despite the recent failure of the Speakeasy ™ speech synthesizer unit, Spreadsheet $ystems' management is bullish on the company. Sales of the company's computer software declined only slightly (10%), which was better than many other companies in the industry. Revenues from the software were $6.75 million, which meant losses were held to only $500,000 in this area. The loss attributable to the new speech synthesizer introduction was $1 million, although management still believes the unit is the best on the market. Total net loss for the year was $1.5 million.

The strength of our marketing and distribution should enable Spreadsheet $ystems to weather our current financial problems and return to profitability within a year. The company is currently engaged in merger discussions with a larger company, which prefers to remain anonymous . . .

DECISION F

The current value of your investment is *$179,550.* Tough luck, your investment is 46% below the average of the experts.

F-11 **Do you keep your money in Spreadsheet $ystems** in the hope that you and the company will make financial sense? (Turn to page 281.)

or

F-12 **Do you play it safe with a 9.5% corporate bond income fund,** returning $17,057? (Turn to page 282.)

After you have made your decision, see the next page for the experts' comments.

THE EXPERTS STRATEGIZE:
F-11. SPREADSHEET $YSTEMS

Chat Morton (High-Risk Expert)—Commentary
Things are getting worse. The net loss for the year was one and a half million dollars. The speech synthesizer introduction was a failure. Sales of financial programs are still declining. To stay with this company at this point is very risky. The promise of a merger is pie in the sky. It appears to be a desperation attempt by the company to keep the stock price up.

Your friend is a hazard to the investment community. He is a rumormonger at best, an economist at worst. This company is going down fast, and you should not be in the stock.

F-12. CORPORATE BOND
INCOME FUND

Jonathan Walker (Risk-Averse Expert)—Commentary
Corporate bond funds typically offer advantages over buying individual corporate bonds because they have diversification and professional management. A professional staff tries to weed out the bonds of weak companies and concentrate on the bonds of strong companies. The yields are typically very good. This bond fund is especially attractive now given the state of the economy, because if interest rates continue to trend down, the fund could do very well in terms of capital appreciation.

(Continued from page 97)

RESULTS:
E-7. CERTIFICATES OF DEPOSIT

THE EXPERTS SPEAK
Georgina Gold

Results. Results. Results. No one argues with results. Your opportunistic strategy of investing only when there is real opportunity has paid off handsomely. You made money in real estate and Spreadsheet Systems and then consolidated in asset management accounts and CDs. If you remain comfortable waiting for the right alternative, do it.

A bank's CD (certificate of deposit) is safe and easy, like driving a Chevy. But is that what you want to do the rest of your life? You made nearly $31,000, which certainly is not bad. In fact, you could go along investing in CDs the rest of your life and never starve. That's exactly what Nathaniel, your banker's husband, recommends. However, when he senses dissatisfaction in your eyes and possible loss of commission in his wallet, he raises another interesting opportunity.

He knows of a friend who is putting on a Broadway play which needs backers. You could put $100,000 into the play (the rest into CDs) and get guaranteed orchestra seats for opening night. No small feat for New York's Great White Way. You remember the movie *The Producers,* in which Zero Mostel, (who was producing the musical "Springtime for Hitler"), hoped to lose money. You wonder whether this play, a musical comedy based on the 1955 Brooklyn Dodgers, is in the same league. You fancy yourself as a patron of the arts and an angel of the theatre. But are you a Broadway mogul? Only time and money will tell.

You look at the numbers, read the Broadway prospectus, and decide.

Bank Investment Advisory Newsletter

The economy continues to flex its muscle. The GNP grew 8% for the year. The index of leading economic indicators also gave the current administration something to cheer about, as the index grew a full 1%, led by the growth in the formation of new businesses and a dip in unemployment claims. Retail sales climbed above the monthly $100 billion level as Sears, J. C. Penney, and K Mart reported banner sales for the year. Inflation fell to 7%, while unemployment remained at 9%. New car sales are above the 10 million annual rate, while steel companies are showing some strength in cutting losses and fighting foreign competition. Corporate profits as a whole grew 13%, while the Dow Jones Industrial Averages set new records. At the same time the prime rate dropped another percent to 11% as rates across the board fell.

Government spending is under control, although conservatives and hawks condemn the recent lids on military spending, while liberals and social welfare advocates call the administration's reductions in the social welfare area unconscionable. Still, taxpayers who are paying less and consumers who are spending more are highly supportive . . .

Champs From Brooklyn

A PROPOSAL

This story of the 1955 Brooklyn Dodgers is about winning and losing against the ultimate enemy, the New York Yankees. A musical comedy with heart and soul, its hero is one of the stars of the Dodgers, who has an inferiority complex about playing baseball in Brooklyn. He meets a Brooklyn girl with a tawdry past, who through love and understanding helps the star to overcome his neuroses and battle the Bronx Bombers. There is compassion and verve in this pennant race romance and sports story. It should be a big hit . . . The producers, whose credits include *Marv Throneberry—An Inside Look at the Man* and *Baseball for Dollars,* have already raised $1.5 million and only need $500,000 more to begin rehearsals. In anticipation of raising this money, the show has been tentatively booked into the Shubert in Boston for September and the Forrest in Philadelphia in October, and it is scheduled to open in New York in November. The producers have already reached agreement with . . . to star in this play. They are also negotiating . . .

DECISION F

The current value of your investment is $357,170. Congratulations, your investment is 8% above the average of the experts.

F-13 **Do you** pay $50 for a Broadway seat and then **invest your money in CDs** yielding 9%, or $32,145? (Turn to page 281.)

or

F-14 **Do you buy the entire show,** get your seats free, and hope the play (with CDs as backup) makes you a financial superstar? (Turn to page 282.)

After you have made your decision, see the next page for the experts' comments.

THE EXPERTS STRATEGIZE: F-13. BROADWAY

Georgina Gold (Opportunistic Expert)—Commentary

This investment is little better than an investment in movie making or a cattle breeding operation. One in maybe ten Broadway plays is successful—and even it probably just breaks even. This is a real long shot. Broadway plays are best invested in by people who have plenty of money to throw away and not too much investment savvy.

F-14. CERTIFICATES OF DEPOSIT

Jonathan Walker (Risk-Averse Expert)—Commentary

CDs are a solid investment. They are monies which are used by large banks and other financial institutions to help fund their normal lending operations. They provide plenty of security and a low but guaranteed yield. They also are insured up to $100,000 by the federal government. As an investor, you should ask whether you want or need a safe, risk-free investment. The answer to this question will determine whether or not you choose CDs.

(Continued from page 97)

RESULTS: E-8. MEDICAL STOCK INDEX OPTIONS

THE EXPERTS SPEAK
Chat Morton

As long as people get sick and need medical care, medical stocks represent good investments. Despite government regulation and cost-control efforts, playing doctor and God is expensive, and people are willing to pay for advances in the health field. The Medtech Index seems to have invested in good companies. The rather mediocre return is the risk you take in any investment. As far as investments go, it seems to be only a matter of time before the index shows signs of real life.

Risk and wealth go hand in hand. However, so do risk and bankruptcy. If you want to earn a greater return, you need to speculate. Take some risks. You chose options—a professional speculator's game. You hired the best. Luckily, you did not lose. In fact, you even made a little money.

You bought options on an index comprised of four medical technology companies, each with excellent prospects. One developed an artificial heart, which sent the stock soaring and could pump money into the company long into the future. The other three are still working in vain on their new organs. As a result, the value of your options increased a modest 6.5%, or just more than $21,000.

Still, Nathaniel advises you to sell your options and invest the proceeds directly in the stocks which make up the fund. Each of the companies is close to a new discovery in medical science, and the market looks very favorably on even the slightest medical advance—such as a cure for hangnails. You think Nathaniel needs a brain transplant, since it could take years before anything concrete happens. Still, if a discovery is made or a new system perfected, you don't want to be left out. The alternative is to buy tax-free municipal funds paying 11.2% (pre-tax equivalent).

You look at the reports, watch "Trapper John" and "St. Elsewhere," and then decide.

Bank Investment Advisory Newsletter

The economy continues to flex its muscle. The GNP grew 8% for the year. The index of leading economic indicators also gave the current administration something to cheer about, as the index grew a full 1%, led by the growth in the formation of new business and a dip in unemployment claims. Retail sales climbed above the monthly $100 billion level as Sears, J. C. Penney, and K Mart reported banner sales for the year. Inflation fell to 7%, while unemployment remained at 9%. New car sales are above the 10 million annual rate, while steel companies are showing some strength in cutting losses and fighting foreign competition. Corporate profits as a whole grew 13%, while the Dow Jones Industrial Averages set new records. At the same time the prime rate dropped another percent to 11% as rates across the board fell.

Government spending is under control, although conservatives and hawks condemn the recent lids on military spending, while liberals and social welfare advocates call the administration's reductions in the social welfare area unconscionable. Still, taxpayers who are paying less and consumers who are spending more are highly supportive . . .

Option ○ ○ ○ ○ ○ ○ ○ ○ ○ ○ ○ ○ ○ ○ ○
Opportunities ○ ○ ○ ○ ○ ○ ○ ○

MEDICAL TECHNOLOGY

Despite only modest gains recorded last year in the Medtech Index Options, this broker continues to recommend them for long-term investment. Heart Pump, Inc., is beginning to report brisk sales of its new artificial heart, while the other three companies in Medtech report significant advances being made in their technology. Each of the companies reported a minimum 10% increase in sales, while Heart Pump's revenues shot up 40%. Net income also was up. Each of the companies is using the increased revenues to support extensive R&D. One of the companies has secured additional financing of $50 million from . . .

DECISION F

The current value of your investment is $347,385. Congratulations, your investment is 5% above the average of the experts.

F-15   *Do you sell your options and buy the stocks,* hoping that medical science and your investment grow together? (Turn to page 281.)

or

F-16   *Do you stay well by investing in a safe, tax-free municipal bond fund,* yielding a pre-tax equivalent of 11.2%, or $38,907? (Turn to page 282.)

After you have made your decision, see the next page for the experts' choices.

THE EXPERTS STRATEGIZE:
F-15. MEDICAL SCIENCE STOCKS

Georgina Gold (Opportunistic Expert) took this alternative.

The medical technology industry continues to be very good. Since my options are expiring, this is a good time to invest in the underlying securities. I made 6.5% last year. There seem to be uptrends in growth in the companies, and they are doing what they are supposed to do in a growth phase: investing a lot of their revenues in extensive R&D. There is tremendous potential here. This is something I'm going to get in on right from the start and stay with for a long time.

F-16. MUNICIPALS

Georgina Gold (Opportunistic Expert) did not take this alternative.

The tax-free municipals have a limited upside potential. I feel with what I know about the medical science industry and with how well those stocks are doing, it is a better bet at this point than just staid municipal bonds.

The relative dollar amounts are interesting. Last year I earned 6.5% on medical science stocks, whereas I could have gained 11.2% on munis. The difference in dollars is only a little more than $15,000. This is insignificant. Therefore, I'm going to take my shot with the medical stocks.

(Continued from page 101)

RESULTS:
E-9. MUNICIPAL MUTUAL FUND

THE EXPERTS SPEAK
Georgina Gold

Your investment strategy leaves little to the imagination. You generally invest in very safe alternatives, with the one exception when you took a chance and lost money. Your return is low to moderate. In the abstract, the strategy is not bad. However, since the economy is now on the move, so should be your investment strategy. Take risks and live a little, unless you're content with your everyday existence.

After T bills, everything looks risky. But still, you need to make your money work for you, so that you don't have to. The only time you lost money was when you invested in options. So you went for the middle road—a relatively safe but moderately yielding municipal mutual fund. You picked the variable rate bonds to try to boast your yield a bit while staying within the limits of safety. You made $16,616, an average pre-tax equivalent return of 11%. Not bad.

But now what? Of course, you could stick with munis. You call up Nathaniel. He says 11% is terrible and suggests you buy real estate—the boom of the '70s. Great, you think, only this is the '80s. He says that real estate is still a great way to make a lot of money fast. His company, in fact, is sponsoring a real estate investment trust which owns and operates several commercial properties. You buy shares in the trust and then earn dividends. In addition, the value of the trust grows as the property appreciates. Since it's well managed and the property is in a prime location, you could make a killing. Sounds great. You ask where the property is located. Nathaniel responds, New Jersey.

You need time to think. You did all right buying munis, but maybe you can get a quick hit from real estate. Besides, New Jersey may be a great place to work, although you wouldn't want to live there. You look over the figures and the reports before you decide.

Bank Investment Advisory Newsletter

The economy continues to flex its muscle. The GNP grew 8% for the year. The index of leading economic indicators also gave the current administration something to cheer about, as the index grew a full 1%, led by the growth in the formation of new businesses and a dip in unemployment claims. Retail sales climbed above the monthly $100 billion level as Sears, J. C. Penney, and K Mart reported banner sales for the year. Inflation fell to 7%, while unemployment remained at 9%. New car sales are above the 10 million annual rate, while steel companies are showing some strength in cutting losses and fighting foreign competition. Corporate profits as a whole grew 13%, while the Dow Jones Industrial Averages set new records. At the same time the prime rate dropped another percent to 11% as rates across the board fell.

Government spending is under control, although conservatives and hawks condemn the recent lids on military spending, while liberals and social welfare advocates call the administration's reductions in the social welfare area unconscionable. Still, taxpayers who are paying less and consumers who are spending more are highly supportive . . .

 ## New Jersey Real Estate Investment Trust

(Not a formal prospectus. Offering can be made only . . .)

This trust is offering shares at $10,000 a unit. The trust owns and operates six commercial properties in New Jersey and manages an additional six others elsewhere. All properties are located within a one-hour drive from New York City, in prime New Jersey commercial areas. The properties are 90% occupied with an excellent base of large and financially sound tenants, including Current Technologies, American Diversified Industries, and Computer Liaisons of New Jersey. This occupancy figure could go higher as the economy improves. The trust guarantees a return of 10%. In addition, property appreciation has averaged 5% to 10% during the last three years.

The properties are ideally located in the heart of New Jersey and . . .

DECISION F

The current value of your investment is $167,669. Tough luck, your investment is 49% below the average of the experts.

F-17 *Do you stick with a municipal mutual fund,* which last year yielded 11%? (Turn to page 281.)

or

F-18 *Do you* become adventuresome and *speculate in New Jersey real estate* on which you hope to build a solid foundation for making your fortune? (Turn to page 282.)

After you have made your decision, see the next page for the experts' comments.

THE EXPERTS STRATEGIZE:
F-17. MUNICIPAL MUTUAL FUND

Jonathan Walker (Risk-Averse Expert)—Commentary
This investment will continue to provide you with all the great tax benefits of a municipal bond. Interest rates continue to fall, so there is little chance of principal erosion. The bonds are professionally managed and the yield is very good. In comparison to speculative real estate, this represents a safe and solid choice.

F-18. NEW JERSEY REAL ESTATE INVESTMENT TRUST

Georgina Gold (Opportunistic Expert)—Commentary
The key elements in a real estate trust are the type of properties owned, the occupancy rates, and, as with everything else in real estate, location, location, location. All properties in this trust are close to New York City. They have 90% occupancy. Should interest rates continue downward and the economy remain robust, vacancies may even go down further. A 10% return is guaranteed. Moreover, there is a good possibility of capital appreciation. This looks like a very good investment opportunity.

(Continued from page 101)

RESULTS:
E-10. DOW JONES FUTURES

THE EXPERTS SPEAK
Chat Morton

Burned again. Every time you try something risky you get burned. The last time you bought options you lost money. This time you lost money on futures. The problem is that options and futures are difficult investments for the nonprofessional to make money on. Does that mean that you should stick with the risk-free alternatives? Not necessarily. It means you should pick your risky investments with great care. Look for value and potential growth. Then close your eyes, cross your fingers, and choose.

If you could predict the future you'd be rich already. Unfortunately you can't, so you're not wealthy. Futures are a tough investment game. You predicted a 15% increase in stock index futures. You also bought on margin, meaning you put only a small amount down. When the index you chose dropped, you were responsible for the loss. Even after considering the gain you made from your money market investment, you still lost 15% of your principal, or nearly $22,700.

You're depressed. You need to make money, not lose it. Your financial prognosticator and advisor, Nathaniel, suggests commodities—specifically, pork bellies. You ask, what *are* pork bellies, anyway? He replies he's never met one but says you can get fat on them. You're kosher. Besides what if they go belly up, you ask. Impossible, says the banker's husband. Somebody always wants pork bellies. This nation is built on them.

Commodities do have an intrinsic appeal. Besides, the alternative for safety is a dull 10% corporate bond. Payment is guaranteed, but your upside potential is limited.

You want to earn more than 10%, but you also don't want to lose money. You look at the numbers and data on commodities, chew the fat, and then make a decision.

Bank Investment Advisory Newsletter

The economy continues to flex its muscle. The GNP grew 8% for the year. The index of leading economic indicators also gave the current administration something to cheer about, as the index grew a full 1%, led by the growth in the formation of new businesses and a dip in unemployment claims. Retail sales climbed above the monthly $100 billion level as Sears, J. C. Penney, and K Mart reported banner sales for the year. Inflation fell to 7%, while unemployment remained at 9%. New car sales are above the 10 million annual rate, while steel companies are showing some strength in cutting losses and fighting foreign competition. Corporate profits as a whole grew 13% while the Dow Jones Industrial Averages set new records. At the same time the prime rate dropped another percent to 11% as rates across the board fell.

Government spending is under control, although conservatives and hawks condemn the recent lids on military spending, while liberals and social welfare advocates call the administration's reductions in the social welfare area unconscionable. Still, taxpayers who are paying less and consumers who are spending more are highly supportive . . .

■STAPLE ITEMS■
A REPORT ON COMMODITIES

PORK BELLIES

The price of pork bellies has been increasing rapidly over last year. When the price of feed shot up during last year's drought, the supply of pork bellies was severely reduced. At the same time, the demand for pork bellies went through the roof. Large traditional purchasers anticipating future shortages increased their inventory, so that pork bellies were in short supply well into the summer. Even when the shortage of feed supplies eased, pork bellies remained in high demand. As a result, the price has not abated this fall and has even risen somewhat. Commodity analysts have been surprised at the strength and the length of this upward price spiral. Future price increases are expected with . . .

DECISION F

The current value of your investment is *$128,395*. Tough luck, your investment is 61% below the average of the experts.

F-19 *Do you buy pork bellies* in the hope of making a killing? (Turn to page 281.)

or

F-20 *Do you* recognize the fickleness of the commodities market and *choose a safe corporate bond* returning 10%, or $12,840? (Turn to page 282.)

After you have made your decision, see the next page for the experts' comments.

THE EXPERTS STRATEGIZE: F-19. PORK BELLY COMMODITY FUTURES

Georgina Gold (Opportunistic Expert)—Commentary

The price of this commodity is going to vary with many different factors: the price of feed, the weather, pig diseases, etc. This is an area that is better left to experts. When you buy a future, you can make a lot of money if prices go up, but if prices go down, you could go broke. Given the complexity of this market, it would be better to avoid investing in this area.

F-20. CORPORATE BONDS

Jonathan Walker (Risk-Averse Expert)—Commentary

Corporate bonds typically are very safe, especially when they are highly rated by a bond rating service. Corporate bonds are debt with a senior claim on a company's assets if the company develops any problems. The 10% interest is good. The only risk is if interest rates go up sharply, which would mean that the price of the bonds would drop. It is possible to reduce this risk by buying shorter term bonds.

The economy seems to favor an investment of this type. Inflation is falling, which should help interest rates. As a result, in the near term there should be little principal risk. In addition, the bonds provide a decent return from interest.

(Continued from page 105)

RESULTS: E-11. GOVERNMENT NOTES

THE EXPERTS SPEAK
Georgina Gold

Time to recoup. After losing handily in the options market, you took a breather and went with the safe, risk-free, government-backed-and-guaranteed 9% notes. Smart move. However, you still have a problem in that you're not making much money, nor do you have a lot of money left to invest after your losses. Therefore, to build your principal you need to look for good but slightly risky growth opportunities. The health and medical fund may be one of them.

So you chose government notes. The only question is what took you so long to get out of options. You were wise not to pick penny stocks. Had you invested half your principal in them you would have lost almost 20% of your money. With the government notes you made 9%, or $10,000. That's almost a 30% difference. Of course, there are people out there earning 30% on their money. Why shouldn't you be one of them?

During your annual checkup, you mention your financial dilemma to your physician, Dr. Geoffrey. He happens to mention that he also is a licensed financial advisor. After all, who knows more about money than doctors? He would be happy to take you as a client and even charge you discount rates, since you're a patient of his. It's obvious he knows how to make money (what doctor doesn't), but does he know how to invest it? Not to worry, says Dr. Geoffrey, making and investing money is his primary occupation. You wince.

Dr. Geoffrey recommends a new mutual fund, made up of medical and drug companies, that will shoot the top off your thermometer. Since medical and drug costs have been the only thing to consistently exceed the inflation rate (with the exception of lunch prices at fancy New York restaurants), you figure this medical/drug fund can't miss. Still, you'd feel better if there was an epidemic or a plague they could cure or eradicate. The other alternative, says Dr. Geoffrey, is to invest in a straight 11% pre-tax equivalent AA-rated municipal bond. In fact, the local government has issued a bond to raise money for a high school gym. It's insured and tax-free, so no need to worry if you want a safe alternative.

You're always healthy, so you're uncertain about the health fund. On the other hand, who ever heard of anything connected with health and medicine being cheap or losing money? But there's always a first time. You look at the data, take your temperature, and then choose.

Bank Investment Advisory Newsletter

The economy continues to flex its muscle. The GNP grew 8% for the year. The index of leading economic indicators also gave the current administration something to cheer about, as the index grew a full 1%, led by the growth in the formation of new businesses and a dip in unemployment claims. Retail sales climbed above the monthly $100 billion level as Sears, J. C. Penney, and K Mart reported banner sales for the year. Inflation fell to 7%, while unemployment remained at 9%. New car sales are above the 10 million annual rate, while steel companies are showing some strength in cutting losses and fighting foreign competition. Corporate profits as a whole grew 13%, while the Dow Jones Industrial Averages set new records. At the same time the prime rate dropped another percent to 11% as rates across the board fell.

Government spending is under control, although conservatives and hawks condemn the recent lids on military spending, while liberals and social welfare advocates call the administration's reductions in the social welfare area unconscionable. Still, taxpayers who are paying less and consumers who are spending more are highly supportive . . .

MERIT-PYNCH INVESTMENT REPORT

HEALTH FUND

The Health Fund is a new mutual fund made up of medical and drug companies. The cost of health care has risen an average of 18% per year for the last five years. Government attempts to control this growth have been successful only to the extent that they have limited the size of the increases to less than 20%. As a result, suppliers and manufacturers of health equipment and drugs have done very well in terms of sales, net income, and profit margins.

The Health Fund was established to take advantage of the growing profits and sales in this area. The fund buys stock in both established companies that are already profitable and new companies with great potential. Recently the fund has chosen to concentrate on new companies. The fund expects to return a yield of 20% + each year, depending on how well these new companies do. However, the investment is risky in that getting new drugs and health equipment approved by the federal authorities is a long and complicated process . . .

DECISION F

The current value of your investment is *$121,794.* Tough luck, your investment is 63% below the average of the experts.

F-21   *Do you invest in an 11% municipal bond,* which will yield $13,397? (Turn to page 283.)

or

F-22   *Do you* believe sickness and money go hand in hand and *invest in the medical/drug mutual fund?* (Turn to page 284.)

After you have made your decision, turn to the next page for the experts' comments.

THE EXPERTS STRATEGIZE: F-21. TAX-FREE MUNICIPALS

Jonathan Walker (Risk-Averse Expert)—Commentary

Why would anyone want to pay taxes? The 7% tax-free income is very good. The bonds are safe and can be easily bought and sold. The primary disadvantage is that if interest rates go up, the value of the bonds goes down. But in any case, the guaranteed pre-tax equivalent yield still is over 11%, year after year. A very safe and wise investment for the cautious at heart.

F-22. MEDICAL DRUG MUTUAL FUND

Chat Morton (High-Risk Expert)—Commentary

This is a fund that is trying to take advantage of the great change in demographics as well as the rising cost of health care. It allows you to put your money in the hands of professional managers, who attempt to select the winners in this high-growth industry. The fund expects to return a yield of 20%+. However, very rarely do you hear people tell you they expect to lose money. The investment is risky since success in the medical and drug field is dependent on new discoveries, long lead times, federal approvals, and so on.

(Continued from page 105)

RESULTS:
E-12. PENNY STOCKS MUTUAL FUND/MUNIS

THE EXPERTS SPEAK
_____ Jonathan Walker _____

Why not apply for bankruptcy now and avoid the trouble of doing it later, when you've lost all your money? Your investments are risky and you have paid the price. You have managed to turn $131,000 into $28,000 in only three short years. Moreoever, this was done in a growing economy. Nice job. A principal lesson on investing and love is *cut short your losses.* Continue with caution. Invest carefully before there is nothing left to invest.

You have the wild look of a crazed investor in your eyes. Anyone who has lost money for a year investing in options and still wants to speculate has to be a little crazy—or know something no one else does. Sure, you could have made 9% or 10% in T bills, but you figured you'd be just as comfortable putting the money under the mattress.

You chose penny stocks, a form of legalized gambling. By putting 50% of your principal in a penny stock fund made of mining companies, you hoped for a copper strike. All they found were empty holes, so you got shafted. The six companies in the fund are not worth much more than the paper they're incorporated on. Your $112,000 investment is now worth only $27,935 having lost 75% of its value.

Still, the write-ups on the future prospects of the companies don't look bad. (Maybe you should invest in the people who do the write-ups rather than the companies themselves.) Any of the six companies could strike it rich. Maybe the companies have a good future; they certainly do not have a good past. On the other hand, T bills also have an attraction—like a guaranteed 8.2% return. The penny stocks are a risky gamble. You reread the fund's prospectus and review the economic data before making a decision.

Bank Investment Advisory Newsletter

The economy continues to flex its muscle. The GNP grew 8% for the year. The index of leading economic indicators also gave the current administration something to cheer about, as the index grew a full 1%, led by the growth in the formation of new businesses and a dip in unemployment claims. Retail sales climbed above the monthly $100 billion level as Sears, J. C. Penney, and K Mart reported banner sales for the year. Inflation fell to 7%, while unemployment remained at 9%. New car sales are above the 10 million annual rate, while steel companies are showing some strength in cutting losses and fighting foreign competition. Corporate profits as a whole grew 13%, while the Dow Jones Industrial Averages set new records. At the same time the prime rate dropped another percent to 11% as rates across the board fell.

Government spending is under control, although conservatives and hawks condemn the recent lids on military spending, while liberals and social welfare advocates call the administration's reductions in the social welfare area unconscionable. Still, taxpayers who are paying less and consumers who are spending more are highly supportive . . .

PRECIOUS METTLE ☐ ☐ ☐
An investment analysis ☐ ☐

GOLD DUST MUTUAL FUND PROSPECTUS

The Gold Dust Fund had a particularly bad year. The fund's capital declined 75%, to $2.5 million. A number of new mining ventures that the fund invested in went bankrupt, while the rest had very slim pickings. The companies that did make discoveries found the price of metal so low that commercial mining was not economically profitable. As a result, the Gold Dust Fund has attempted to weed out unprofitable ventures and concentrate a heavier percentage of its capital in a few promising companies. Three were chosen, each of which showed a small profit last year but has great promise. We believe a more selective strategy will be successful. The prospects for each company . . .

DECISION F

The current value of your investment is $27,935. Tough luck, your investment is 92% below the average of the experts.

F-23 **Do you** risk your future on the bit of a drill and **keep your money in the penny mining stock fund?** (Turn to page 283.)

or

F-24 **Do you mine U.S. T bills,** which guarantee you a find of 8.2%, or $2,291, after one year? (Turn to page 284.)

After you have made your decision, turn to the next page for the experts' comments.

THE EXPERTS STRATEGIZE:
F-23. PENNY MINING STOCKS

Georgina Gold (Opportunistic Expert)—Commentary

As with most penny stocks, the underlying companies are quite weak. In this case the track record of the Gold Dust Mutual Fund has been dismal. Its assets decreased 75% last year. A number of the companies went bankrupt, while the remaining companies had very poor years.

This would be an out-and-out speculation. You're betting on the companies' finding gold and mining it profitably. You're also betting the price of gold will go up. Finally, you're betting on the fund management to pick winners—which it hasn't done in the past. I would not be a betting man or woman if I were you.

F-24. T BILLS

Jonathan Walker (Risk-Averse Expert)—Commentary

T bills are absolutely the safest investment to put your money into. There is no risk on the principal. Your interest will be paid by the U.S. government. This is the place to put money when you don't really know what you want to do with it, yet you want to make sure you have it when you want it. Money can be withdrawn from T bills at any time. The markets are extremely liquid.

(Continued from page 109)

RESULTS:
E-13. TIME DEPOSITS

THE EXPERTS SPEAK
Chat Morton

The growth of your principal has been steady but not spectacular. You have continually opted for the risk-averse alternative, and your inheritance is now a bit over $175,000. Hardly great expectations. Basically, you have made a clear-cut choice, despite the availability of opportunity for greater returns in a growing and vibrant economy. Still, dreams die hard. You would be wise to consider other options, especially those which are more risky and offer greater returns.

At least you're consistent. Not rich, but consistent. Again you made a respectable 10%, or $16,000, in the time deposits. You have never lost money investing this way. However, it was a mistake to ignore the stock tip. The new laundry detergent of Washout, Inc., was a fabulous success. As a result, the stock tripled in value. Your 10% gain could have been 200%. Investing can be a dirty business.

Nathaniel, your banker's husband, drops by. He hears from his wife that you are thinking of withdrawing your funds from the time deposits, so he's come by to offer advice. You think he smells money. He says of course you could renew the time deposits, as you have done four of the last five times, but isn't it a bit early to retire your money, especially since it's earning only $16,000 a year?

Maybe you should consider convertible bonds, which offer safety plus growth potential. These bonds are debt of a company which can be exchanged or converted into a set number of shares until the bonds mature. The interest rate is only 2 points below time deposits, but at least there is the possibility of making a killing. He recommends a AA-rated company called Current Technologies.

You wonder whether now is the time to gamble or whether you should stay with the steady but profitable money market fund. You look over the reports and data before you decide.

Bank Investment Advisory Newsletter

The economy continues to flex its muscle. The GNP grew 8% for the year. The index of leading economic indicators also gave the current administration something to cheer about, as the index grew a full 1%, led by the growth in the formation of new businesses and a dip in unemployment claims. Retail sales climbed above the monthly $100 billion level as Sears, J. C. Penney, and K Mart reported banner sales for the year. Inflation fell to 7%, while unemployment remained at 9%. New car sales are above the 10 million annual rate, while steel companies are showing some strength in cutting losses and fighting foreign competition. Corporate profits as a whole grew 13%, while the Dow Jones Industrial Averages set new records. At the same time the prime rate dropped another percent to 11% as rates across the board fell.

Government spending is under control, although conservatives and hawks condemn the recent lids on military spending, while liberals and social welfare advocates call the administration's reductions in the social welfare area unconscionable. Still, taxpayers who are paying less and consumers who are spending more are highly supportive . . .

Street Scene Magazine

"STRATEGY IS THE KEY TO SUCCESS FOR CURRENT TECHNOLOGIES"

. . . Sales and profits continue to increase in the high double-digit range. Abetted by a large order from Sears and Penney, the consumer electronics division is booming.

Industrial products, tried-and-true, have found their way into numerous space and military hardware. Current Technologies management forecasts growth in revenues and profits in the 20% ballpark. There does not seem to be any reason to doubt that. The company is strategically well positioned against foreign and domestic competitors . . .

DECISION F

The current value of your investment is *$177,214*. Tough luck, your investment is 46% below the average of the experts.

F-25   *Do you* stick with a good thing and *reinvest in 10% time deposits* paying a guaranteed $17,721? (Turn to page 283.)

or

F-26   *Do you gamble on 8% convertible bonds* in the hope of increasing your fortune? (Turn to page 284.)

After you have made your decision, turn to the next page for the experts' choices.

THE EXPERTS STRATEGIZE: F-25. TIME DEPOSITS

Jonathan Walker (Risk-Averse Expert) took this alternative.

You can't make me part with my money; I'm no fool. My fortune is growing by leaps and bounds. I'm up to $177,000, and now I can get another $18,000 for doing nothing. I'll make almost as much from my investment as I will from my salary. I'll be able to quit soon if I keep this up. I'm in no rush to join the jet set. I like my money.

F-26. CONVERTIBLE BONDS

Jonathan Walker (Risk-Averse Expert) did not take this alternative.

The price of convertible bonds varies with interest rates and the underlying stock. If the stock goes down, I'm going to be out some dough. It doesn't make any sense for me to gamble on 8% convertible bonds when I've got a sure thing in 10% time deposits.

(Continued from page 109)

RESULTS E-14. WASHOUT, INC.

THE EXPERTS SPEAK
Georgina Gold

When you wish upon a star. After taking the conservative but safe route for four years, your inheritance had grown $61,000. In one bold move you made over $300,000. If you invest in the right company at the right time you can make a fortune. Washout, Inc., had an outstanding product. Many successful companies have been built that way—Polaroid, Apple, etc. If you feel that you can spot or pick out the successful companies before they become successful, never do anything else.

Cleanliness is next to God—and your wallet. The new laundry detergent was everything that Nathaniel said it was. Sales were limited only by production capacity at the factory. Washout, Inc., reported a tenfold increase in revenues and profits. The value of the stock tripled. Your $161,000 investment suddenly is worth $483,000. No ring around the collar for you.

You call up Nathaniel to thank him for the tip. You even offer to take him out for lunch at the restaurant of his choice. Four drinks and $225 later, Nathaniel asks whether you plan to keep your Washout, Inc., stock, given the company's management and production problems. You almost choke. With almost a half million dollars in that little Philadelphia company, you have more than a passing interest. Nathaniel pulls out a magazine article which compares investing in the company to riding on the *Titanic* — it's great while it lasts.

You look for the phone in the restaurant while asking Nathaniel to sell your shares and buy a safe 9.5% corporate bond in the largest, safest multinational conglomerate he can find. Nathaniel says not so fast. Pay the check, go home and watch the market report on TV, think about it for a few hours, and then decide.

Bank Investment Advisory Newsletter

The economy continues to flex its muscle. The GNP grew 8% for the year. The index of leading economic indicators also gave the current administration something to cheer about, as the index grew a full 1%, led by the growth in the formation of new businesses and a dip in unemployment claims. Retail sales climbed above the monthly $100 billion level as Sears, J. C. Penney, and K Mart reported banner sales for the year. Inflation fell to 7%, while unemployment remained at 9%. New car sales are above the 10 million annual rate, while steel companies are showing some strength in cutting losses and fighting foreign competition. Corporate profits as a whole grew 13%, while the Dow Jones Industrial Averages set new records. At the same time the prime rate dropped another percent to 11% as rates across the board fell.

Government spending is under control, although conservatives and hawks condemn the recent lids on military spending, while liberals and social welfare advocates call the administration's reductions in the social welfare area unconscionable. Still, taxpayers who are paying less and consumers who are spending more are highly supportive. . .

THE NOW JONES DIGEST WITH JIM TENKAY

Washout, Inc., last year introduced a great new laundry detergent nationwide. It truly was better than anything else on the market, and as a result it captured an incredible 7% of the

category in only one year. The company tripled in size almost overnight. An old factory was bought and converted to add production capacity to the current plant, and the company ran three shifts.

But growth does have its problems. One of the inventors of the product filed a lawsuit against the company over her share of the royalties. Quality control was not up to standard. The company is

now at a crossroads. It will either be highly successful in the future or, like the Titanic . . .

DECISION F

The current value of your investment is *$483,312*. Congratulations, your investment is 46% above the average of the experts.

F-27   *Do you hold on to your Washout, Inc., shares,* hoping that the company will continue to make money and not clean you out? (Turn to page 283.)

or

F-28   *Do you sell your shares and return to* safe but comfortable 9.5% *corporate bonds,* returning $45,915? (Turn to page 284.)

After you have made your decision, turn to the next page for the experts' comments.

THE EXPERTS STRATEGIZE: F-27. WASHOUT, INC.

Georgina Gold (Opportunistic Expert)—Commentary

The future of this company is difficult to predict. While it has had outstanding success in developing and marketing a new product, there are trouble signs in the wings. The attention of management is being diverted by a lawsuit, which may be very costly and time-consuming to resolve. In addition, any new product can be destroyed by poor quality control. On the other hand, the company does have the basic essentials for a highly successful growth company—a great product, good marketing, and sufficient financial resources. Whether the company will grow in the future at the same rate (a tenfold increase in sales and profits) is highly doubtful, but even a slow growth rate still would be spectacular.

F-28. CORPORATE BONDS

Jonathan Walker (Risk-Averse Expert)—Commentary

Corporate bonds typically are very safe. They are debt with a senior claim on a company's assets if the company develops any problems. The 9.5% interest is good. The only risk is if interest rates go up sharply then the price of the bonds will drop. It is possible to reduce this risk by buying shorter term bonds.

The economy seems to favor an investment of this type. Inflation is falling, which should help interest rates. As a result, in the near term there should be little principal risk. In addition, the bonds provide a decent return from interest.

(Continued from page 113)

RESULTS:
E-15. DOW JONES INDEX FUND

THE EXPERTS SPEAK
Chat Morton

Go with the flow. When the market is on an upswing, invest in it. You were smart to pick an index fund, which is far less risky than trying to pick individual winners. Even the high-flier fund couldn't match the Dow Jones Averages for performance. The economy continues to show signs of strength and vitality without becoming overheated. You gambled last time and made money. In fact, 3% more than you made the year before in a safe alternative.

You played the law of averages and got a better-than-average return. You stuck with the Dow Jones Index Fund. With the economy improving and companies reporting record profits, the index gained a strong 17%, or $28,000. As it turned out, this is a lot better than the 6% return from the high flier mutual fund you were considering. In fact, the high-flier fund could be more aptly called a low-flier fund.

You've made good money on the market index fund. The question now is, should you continue? Nathaniel, an expert in matters of the wallet, says you can always stay with the index if you want to. However, given the increase in the value of your investment to almost $200,000, you should really consider tax-free munis. Munis are bonds or debt of local or state governments. Because one governmental unit cannot normally tax another, the munis are tax-free. Since the higher your income bracket, the higher your tax rate, tax-free investments provide greater savings the more money you make. These tax-free municipals offer a very competitive 7%, or 11.2% pre-tax equivalent return. Moreover, this return is guaranteed. You ask, but aren't you limiting your upside potential with munis? (Upside potential is a word you picked up in an investment primer). Yes, says Nathaniel, but that is the price you pay for safety.

You wonder whether you're willing to pay that price at twenty-nine years of age. Maybe now is the time to gamble before you're old at thirty-five. You look over the data and decide.

Bank Investment Advisory Newsletter

The economy continues to flex its muscle. The GNP grew 8% for the year. The index of leading economic indicators also gave the current administration something to cheer about, as the index grew a full 1%, led by the growth in the formation of new businesses and a dip in unemployment claims. Retail sales climbed above the monthly $100 billion level as Sears, J. C. Penney, and K Mart reported banner sales for the year. Inflation fell to 7%, while unemployment remained at 9%. New car sales are above the 10 million annual rate, while steel companies are showing some strength in cutting losses and fighting foreign competition. Corporate profits as a whole grew 13% while the Dow Jones Industrial Averages set new records. At the same time the prime rate dropped another percent to 11% as rates across the board fell.

Government spending is under control, although conservatives and hawks condemn the recent lids on military spending, while liberals and social welfare advocates call the administration's reductions in the social welfare area unconscionable. Still, taxpayers who are paying less and consumers who are spending more are highly supportive . . .

T. KITZINGER'S MARKET OUTLOOK

The market has never been stronger. Trading is heavy with 100-million-share days no longer uncommon. The economy seems for the moment to be under control. Inflation is in check, while even interest rates have declined. The Dow Jones Averages have rallied in the past three months. The Standard and Poor's 500 gained 10 points over the last quarter. A composite index shows losers are now a small . . . For the next six to nine months, economists at the major brokerage houses are predicting continued strong performance with some big winners and very few losers. Institutional buying continues to be heavy, especially in blue-chip and energy issues. Attractive stocks to watch are . . .

DECISION F

The current value of your investment is *$193,586*. Tough luck, your investment is 42% below the average of the experts.

F-29 *Do you continue to play the market averages by buying the Dow Jones Index Fund,* which looks very good in a growing economy? (Turn to page 283.)

or

F-30 *Do you* now consider yourself a person of means who needs to *invest only in tax-free instruments such as munis* paying 11.2% pre-tax equivalent, or $21,682? (Turn to page 284.)

After you have made your decision, turn to the next page for the experts' comments.

THE EXPERTS STRATEGIZE:
F-29. DOW JONES INDEX FUND

Georgina Gold (Opportunistic Expert)—Commentary

The Dow Jones Index Fund continues to look like a very good bet. The economy is really starting to grow, government spending is under control, and retail sales are up. As a result, the market is doing extremely well. Volume is heavy. Institutional buying is continuing to drive prices higher. There really is no reason to expect things to change. This is a good investment.

F-30. TAX-FREE MUNICIPALS

Jonathan Walker (Risk-Averse Expert)—Commentary

Why would anyone want to pay taxes? The 7% tax-free income is very good. The bonds are safe and can be easily bought and sold. The primary disadvantage is that if interest rates go up, the value of the bonds goes down. But in any case, the guaranteed pre-tax equivalent yield still is over 11%, year after year. A very safe and wise investment for the cautious at heart.

(Continued from page 113)

RESULTS:
E-16. HIGH-FLIER FUND

THE EXPERTS SPEAK
Chat Morton

Your investments have gotten riskier, and you finally paid the price. After making nothing less than 11% (and that was with T bills), the high-flier fund floundered. But that is investing. If there was no risk, then there would be no high returns. Despite the low return, the computer fund did seem like a good investment with good companies in a growing industry in a growing economy. Too bad, no one wins all the time.

Anything that can't lose, will lose (Murphy's first law of investing). The high-flier mutual fund is no exception. Instead of gaining in the predicted double-digit range (20% to 30%), the fund returned a pauperly 6%, or $10,000. Hardly enough for you to live like a king—or even a page. In comparison, the Dow Jones Index Fund you passed over gained 17%, or double the sure thing. So much for your luck and investment prowess.

Your first inclination is to run and buy safe CDs—no risk and 10% guaranteed return. Still, you keep telling yourself, don't panic. Because one investment doesn't work doesn't mean you're broke. You call up Nathaniel, the financial Mr. Answer, for advice. He recommends a well-balanced portfolio of stock options and T bills. Even if you knew what a portfolio was, you'd still be concerned. Aren't options highly risky, you ask. Generally, yes, he responds, but the company he is recommending, American Diversified Industries, is growing by leaps and bounds. You ask, does that mean it's making money? Of course, he says.

You're not so sure. You lost once on a gamble; maybe you should take the CDs. However, wouldn't it be nice not to have to argue over who pays the tip each time you go out to eat with friends? Maybe options aren't so bad. You review the reports and make a decision.

Bank Investment Advisory Newsletter

The economy continues to flex its muscle. The GNP grew 8% for the year. The index of leading economic indicators also gave the current administration something to cheer about, as the index grew a full 1%, led by the growth in the formation of new businesses and a dip in unemployment claims. Retail sales climbed above the monthly $100 billion level as Sears, J. C. Penney, and K Mart reported banner sales for the year. Inflation fell to 7%, while unemployment remained at 9%. New car sales are above the 10 million annual rate, while steel companies are showing some strength in cutting losses and fighting foreign competition. Corporate profits as a whole grew 13%, while the Dow Jones Industrial Averages set new records. At the same time the prime rate dropped another percent to 11% as rates across the board fell.

Government spending is under control, although conservatives and hawks condemn the recent lids on military spending, while liberals and social welfare advocates call the administration's reductions in the social welfare area unconscionable. Still, taxpayers who are paying less and consumers who are spending more are highly supportive . . .

Street Scene Magazine

"CONGLOMERATES CAN WORK"

American Diversified Industries' fast food and financial operations continue to grow at a breakneck pace. Both experienced growth in revenue and sales of 30%+. If the rather staid, conservative fashion line had kept pace, the company would have reported an even larger profit. Sales topped $800 million, while net income rose to $65 million. The fast food operation is thinking of expanding into the Southwest. Its management has already acquired 10 prime locations in Texas. The financial services division has bought an investment advisory house, which means the company can offer complete investment services. The only note of caution is a question as to how long this great growth can continue . . . American Diversified Industries is recommended as a "buy" for the short term by the brokerage house of . . .

DECISION F

The current value of your investment is *$175,385*. Tough luck, your investment is 47% below the average of the experts.

F-31 **Do you** save your pennies and **buy 10% CDs** yielding $17,539? (Turn to page 285.)

or

F-32 **Do you buy options/T bills** and hope your dreams come true? (Turn to page 286.)

After you have made your decision, turn to the next page for the experts' comments.

THE EXPERTS STRATEGIZE:
F-31. CERTIFICATES OF DEPOSIT

Jonathan Walker (Risk-Averse Expert)—Commentary

CDs are a solid investment. They are monies which are used by large banks and other financial institutions to help fund their normal lending operations. They provide plenty of security and a low but guaranteed yield. They also are insured up to $100,000 by the federal government. As an investor, you should ask whether you want or need a safe, risk-free investment. The answer to this question will determine whether or not you choose CDs.

F-32. OPTIONS/T BILLS

Georgina Gold (Opportunistic Expert)—Commentary

This is an interesting alternative because it combines a very risky investment with a very safe one. The options on American Diversified Industries stock are a good speculation, since the company is doing well. Operations are expanding. Sales are growing. Net income is up. If this trend continues, the stock price could go up. The options then might be a tremendous investment.

But again, options are risky, because when they expire you have nothing. The Treasury bills, on the other hand, offer you the safety and security you don't have in the options. The combination of the two might be worthwhile if you have a lot of confidence in American Diversified Industries.

(Continued from page 117)

RESULTS:
E-17. GINNIE MAES

THE EXPERTS SPEAK
Georgina Gold

Money begets money. Once you made your fortune in Spreadsheet Systems, you took your money and put it into safe investments. Ginnie Maes is your latest choice from the *Smart Investor's Handbook.* The yield is very good, and it's backed by the U.S. government. Certainly with the economy growing, there are other opportunities out there, but it will be hard to beat a 12.5% safe return. Your move.

You may trust in God, but you invest in the federal government. The federally guaranteed Ginnie Maes are backed by the FHA and the VA. The return is a stable 12% plus certain other benefits, such as monthly reinvestment of the principal, bringing the total package to 12.5%, or a very nice $48,981. In addition, you were wise not to invest in speculative tax-free energy bonds, because one of the municipal power authorities declared insolvency. This sent shockwaves throughout the municipal bond market, which resulted in lower value for bonds in general.

Sticking with Ginnie Maes seems like a good idea, even if the name doesn't sound much like high-grade government bonds. On the other hand, with almost a half million dollars in your pocket, maybe now is the time to live and invest more dangerously. You call up your cousin Leonard for advice. He suggests convertible bonds from a company called Current Technologies, which is a multibillion dollar manufacturer of electrical products. The bonds pay 8% and are convertible to shares should the stock grow 10% or more. The only question is how high the stock will go.

You've done well with Ginnie Maes, but maybe now you should turn on to an electrical company. You look at the data before you make your decision.

Bank Investment Advisory Newsletter

The economy continues to flex its muscle. The GNP grew 8% for the year. The index of leading economic indicators also gave the current administration something to cheer about, as the index grew a full 1%, led by the growth in the formation of new businesses and a dip in unemployment claims. Retail sales climbed above the monthly $100 billion level as Sears, J. C. Penney, and K Mart reported banner sales for the year. Inflation fell to 7%, while unemployment remained at 9%. New car sales are above the 10 million annual rate, while steel companies are showing some strength in cutting losses and fighting foreign competition. Corporate profits as a whole grew 13%, while the Dow Jones Industrial Averages set new records. At the same time the prime rate dropped another percent to 11% as rates across the board fell.

Government spending is under control, although conservatives and hawks condemn the recent lids on military spending, while liberals and social welfare advocates call the administration's reductions in the social welfare area unconscionable. Still, taxpayers who are paying less and consumers who are spending more are highly supportive . . .

Street Scene Magazine

"STRATEGY IS THE KEY TO SUCCESS FOR CURRENT TECHNOLOGIES"

. . . Sales and profits continue to increase in the high double-digit range. Abetted by a large order from Sears and Penney, the consumer electronics division is booming.

Industrial products, tried-and-true, have found their way into numerous space and military hardware. Current Technologies management forecasts growth in revenues and profits in the 20% ballpark. There does not seem to be any reason to doubt that. The company is strategically well positioned against foreign and domestic competitors . . .

DECISION F

The current value of your investment is $440,831. Congratulations, your investment is 33% above the average of the experts.

F-33 **Do you keep your money secure in 12.5% federally guaranteed government mortgages (Ginnie Maes)** yielding $55,104. (Turn to page 285.)

or

F-34 **Do you speculate on Current Technologies convertible bonds** with an 8% downside risk and no limit on your financial future? (Turn to page 286.)

After you have made your decision, turn to the next page for the experts' comments.

THE EXPERTS STRATEGIZE:
F-33. GINNIE MAES

Jonathan Walker (Risk-Averse Expert)—Commentary

Ginnie Maes continue to be a good, safe investment. The yield still is 2 to 3 points better than certificates of deposit and even higher than that on government notes. All this and it's backed by the full faith and credit of the U.S. government. Since interest rates in general are declining, the risk of principal erosion is small. The question is, why speculate when you can make 12 1/2% on your money, risk-free?

F-34. CONVERTIBLE BONDS

Georgina Gold (Opportunistic Expert)—Commentary

Convertible bonds have two main advantages: a guaranteed yield, which makes it like a bond, but also upside potential should the stock rally. Current Technologies is a good-looking stock. Sales and profits are up. There are large new orders from major retail chains, and 20% growth is predicted for the coming year. As a result, there are good upside possibilities in terms of bond appreciation, while the bond yield still will protect you on the downside.

(Continued from page 117)

RESULTS:
E-18. NUCLEAR POWER AUTHORITY BOND FUND

THE EXPERTS SPEAK
Georgina Gold

Easy come, easy to. What's horrible is that you lost a lot of money on what was supposed to be a safe investment. You learned that no investment is completely risk-free, especially high-yielding energy bonds. There is a reason that the interest rate on the bonds is higher than the prime rate. So now you have to make up all the money you lost. You can recoup slowly on CDs or play the commodities game and try to recoup your wealth quickly. Commodities can make money fast, but they can also lose it even faster. There is no right answer.

There is no such thing as a free lunch, especially one sponsored by the government. One of those supposedly safe tax-free bond issues defaulted. The bond was issued to raise capital to build a nuclear power plant that did not go on-line. A combination of safety factors, public opposition, and NRC licensing difficulties killed the beast. Hence, instead of making your normal 11% tax-and-risk-free, you actually lost money—and a lot of it. Exactly 80%, or $313,480, evaporated. Even the government is not perfect. Of course, there is solace in that the courts returned 20¢ on the dollar to you.

You quickly call your advisor Leonard to find out what happened. He's on the phone but will call you back in a few minutes. Three days later, he returns your call. Your remember getting different treatment when you were a winner. After the normal apologies for not getting back to you sooner and for having made a recommendation which cost you over $300,000, Leonard now suggests commodities. If you're going to lose money, you might as well do it in style. There is a new commodities index of three food staples: corn, wheat, and soy beans. Leonard advises putting half your money in commodities and the other half in CDs. Of course, you could always put all your money in 9.5% CDs, he says, but why not live a little? This is sound advice from the same man who sold you bankrupt municipals.

You review the data and decide.

Bank Investment Advisory Newsletter

The economy continues to flex its muscle. The GNP grew 8% for the year. The index of leading economic indicators also gave the current administration something to cheer about, as the index grew a full 1%, led by the growth in the formation of new businesses and a dip in unemployment claims. Retail sales climbed above the monthly $100 billion level as Sears, J. C. Penney, and K Mart reported banner sales for the year. Inflation fell to 7%, while unemployment remained at 9%. New car sales are above the 10 million annual rate, while steel companies are showing some strength in cutting losses and fighting foreign competition. Corporate profits as a whole grew 13%, while the Dow Jones Industrial Averages set new records. At the same time the prime rate dropped another percent to 11% as rates across the board fell.

Government spending is under control, although conservatives and hawks condemn the recent lids on military spending, while liberals and social welfare advocates call the administration's reductions in the social welfare area unconscionable. Still, taxpayers who are paying less and consumers who are spending more are highly supportive . . .

■STAPLE ITEMS■
A REPORT ON COMMODITIES

The market for grains this year is strong. After a serious drought last spring and an increase in the government's acreage reduction program, the supply of wheat, corn, and soybeans is down drastically. At the same time, the demand is up. Foreign governments, especially the Soviet Union, have been hard hit by crop failures and bad weather conditions. To reduce food and feed grain shortages, foreign countries have turned to the U.S. to fill their staple needs. Given that the forecast for the coming year shows only moderate increases (5% to 10%) in crop harvests—wheat (2.5 billion bushels), corn (5 billion bushels), and soybeans (2 billion bushels)— the price should be significantly higher. However, if the government decides to cut back on its acreage reduction program, prices could be somewhat moderated.

DECISION F

The current value of your investment is $78,370. Tough luck, your investment is 76% below the average of the experts.

F-35 **Do you** go for caviar and champagne (if you eat at all) and **buy commodities and CDs?** (Turn to page 285.)

or

F-36 **Are you strictly a bread-and-butter person who invests in 9.5% CDs** paying $7,445? (Turn to page 286.)

After you have made your decision, turn to the next page for the experts' comments.

THE EXPERTS STRATEGIZE:
F-35. GRAIN COMMODITIES

Chat Morton (High-Risk Expert)—Commentary

The commodities markets are a professional game with losers outnumbering winners by four to one. Although soy bean, wheat, and corn are staples and there is constant demand for them throughout the world, prices tend to fluctuate wildly based on supply and government restrictions on their movements. This is a high-risk game. There is a great chance you will get burned and not have any bread to eat yourself. Stick with Wheaties, the Breakfast of Champions, and leave commodities to the pros.

F-36. CERTIFICATES OF DEPOSIT

Jonathan Walker (Risk-Averse Expert)—Commentary

CDs are a solid investment. They are monies which are used by large banks and other financial institutions to help fund their normal lending operations. They provide plenty of security and a low but guaranteed yield. They also are insured up to $100,000 by the federal government. As an investor, you should ask yourself whether you want or need a safe, risk-free investment. The answer to this question will determine whether or not you choose CDs.

(Continued from page 121)

RESULTS:
E-19. SUN BELT REAL ESTATE

THE EXPERTS SPEAK
Chat Morton

Landed gentry. You like the idea of making a lot of money on your property. Your 75% gain is great, especially in light of the beating you took in options last year. Some investments which are labeled "risky" are truly risky, while other supposedly risky investments, like real estate, seem to outperform the market year after year. As long as you avoid buying real estate in Cleveland or Detroit, you should continue to make money owning land.

Real estate has always been a favorite investment of the wealthy. You can earn income and appreciation with unlimited growth potential, unless of course you buy in a garden spot such as New Jersey or Upstate New York. The investment trust you put your money in considers properties only in the Sun Belt. As a result, the trust has done very well. This year is no exception. In fact, real estate took off. The investment returned 13% interest, plus the trust increased 62% in value, for a tremendous 75% gain, or $263,340. Why would you ever do anything else?

Maybe you should visit your properties in the Sun Belt and write the trip off on your taxes as a business expense. Sounds great. That alone may be reason enough to keep your money in the trust. On the other hand, you also want to make money, and you wonder whether it's possible for the trust to return even 75% next year. However, you figure even a 50% increase wouldn't be bad. But what if one of the properties fails? It is not impossible. Then your dreams of wealth fade. You become nervous and concerned.

To ease your mind, you call up your cousin Leonard, financial advisor to the semiwealthy. He says if you're concerned about the risk in real estate, you could always invest in a safe corporate bond paying 10%. But if you want to build your fortune, nothing beats the allure of owning land.

You look out the window of your apartment as you review the information for a decision.

Bank Investment Advisory Newsletter

The economy continues to flex its muscle. The GNP grew 8% for the year. The index of leading economic indicators also gave the current administration something to cheer about, (to make consistent throughout) as the index grew a full 1%, led by the growth in the formation of new businesses and a dip in unemployment claims. Retail sales climbed above the monthly $100 billion level as Sears, J. C. Penney, and K Mart reported banner sales for the year. Inflation fell to 7%, while unemployment remained at 9%. New car sales are above the 10 million annual rate, while steel companies are showing some strength in cutting losses and fighting foreign competition. Corporate profits as a whole grew 13%, while the Dow Jones Industrial Averages set new records. At the same time the prime rate dropped another percent to 11% as rates across the board fell.

Government spending is under control, although conservatives and hawks condemn the recent lids on military spending, while liberals and social welfare advocates call the administration's reductions in the social welfare area unconscionable. Still, taxpayers who are paying less and consumers who are spending more are highly supportive

MERIT-PYNCH INVESTMENT REPORT

SUN BELT INVESTMENT TRUST

Sun Belt Investment Trust (SBIT) continues to outperform other real estate investment opportunities and other options by a wide margin. Last year, SBIT showed a 75% gain through long-term appreciation, cash distributions from operations, and equity accumulation through mortgage reduction. This year the Sun Belt Trust has expanded its holdings in the booming commercial real estate markets of Dallas and Houston. Expected yield this year should reach at least 50%, or the average of the last three years. This year the Sun Belt Investment Trust is offering a new high-income, high-appreciation . . .

DECISION F

The current value of your investment is *$614,460*. Congratulations, your investment is 86% above the average of the experts.

F-37 *Do you* stay with your roots and *keep your money in the real estate trust?* (Turn to page 285.)

or

F-38 *Do you* go for complete safety and *invest in a 10% corporate bond* for a gain of $61,446? (Turn to page 286.)

After you have made your decision, turn to the next page for the experts' comments.

THE EXPERTS STRATEGIZE: F-37. SUN BELT REAL ESTATE TRUST

Georgina Gold (Opportunistic Expert)—Commentary

There has been an expansion in this investment trust. While last year's performance was good, there is much greater investment now in the Dallas and Houston markets, which have been booming. Real estate tends to be highly cyclical, and overproduction of units can drive down prices. However, this still should be a tremendous investment. It will be necessary, though, to monitor the company carefully to make sure it doesn't overexpand into glutted markets.

F-38. CORPORATE BONDS

Jonathan Walker (Risk-Averse Expert)—Commentary

Corporate bonds typically are very safe. They are debt with a senior claim on a company's assets if the company develops any problems. The 10% interest is good. The only risk is if interest rates go up sharply, then the price of the bonds will drop. It is possible to reduce this risk by buying shorter term bonds.

The economy seems to favor an investment of this type. Inflation is falling, which should help interest rates. As a result, in the near term there should be little principal risk. In addition, the bonds provide a decent return from interest.

(Continued from page 121)

RESULTS:
E-20. CORPORATE BOND
INCOME FUND

THE EXPERTS SPEAK
Chat Morton

You made a lot of money gambling until you found out that no hayride lasts forever. You lost money on options and then invested in a 10% bond fund. Your caution in investing in a bond fund, given that the economy is growing and there are real estate opportunities out there, was not wise. Over the long run you have almost quadrupled your initial inheritance. You did it by speculating. Speculating is a risky strategy, but it's great if it works. Go with your strengths.

You made your fortune gambling. But why should you lose it the same way? Therefore, you decided to invest in a fixed rate 10% mutual fund to regain some of the losses you suffered in options. You made $35,112. Not too shabby. Unfortunately, had you invested in real estate you could have made a killing—a 75% gain on your investment, or $263,340. Still, you're not unhappy, just unlucky—relatively speaking.

You call up Leonard, crying that you missed the real estate deal of the century. What can you do to make it up? Diamonds, responds Leonard. The world supply is limited, while the demand is great. As a result, diamonds offer great rewards. What's the catch, you ask. Leonard says that either the supply can be upset by dumping by the Russians or the demand can be reduced by high interest rates. Then the allure of diamonds fades quickly. But that is unlikely to happen, assures Leonard. You think everything would be fine if Liz Taylor were still being given diamonds by her current husband. If you're unsure, he says, then put your money into an asset management account paying 8% and wait.

You hesitate, think of the fabulous wealth you don't have, read the reports, and decide.

Bank Investment Advisory Newsletter

The economy continues to flex its muscle. The GNP grew 8% for the year. The index of leading economic indicators also gave the current administration something to cheer about, as the index grew a full 1%, led by the growth in the formation of new businesses and a dip in unemployment claims. Retail sales climbed above the monthly $100 billion level as Sears, J. C. Penney, and K Mart reported banner sales for the year. Inflation fell to 7%, while unemployment remained at 9%. New car sales are above the 10 million annual rate, while steel companies are showing some strength in cutting losses and fighting foreign competition. Corporate profits as a whole grew 13%, while the Dow Jones Industrial Averages set new records. At the same time the prime rate dropped another percent to 11% as rates across the board fell.

Government spending is under control, although conservatives and hawks condemn the recent lids on military spending, while liberals and social welfare advocates call the administration's reductions in the social welfare area unconscionable. Still, taxpayers who are paying less and consumers who are spending more are highly supportive . . .

PRECIOUS METTLE □□□
An investment analysis□□

DIAMONDS— INVESTMENT OUTLOOK

After a period of skyrocketing prices brought on by increased demand and curtailed production, many analysts are urging caution to investors for fear the price structure may fall. Some price erosion was noted in the third quarter, although the fourth quarter of the year was particularly strong. World production increased by 25% and is expected to remain at a higher level for the foreseeable future. Prices could drop if the Russians sell off large quantities to finance military adventures. As a result, most analysts advise a "hold" policy, while a few urge liquidation for the long term and are "neutral" for the short term . . . Two prominent analysts, however, advocate increased holdings as a means . . .

DECISION F

The current value of your investment is *$386,232.* Congratulations, your investment is 17% above the average of the experts.

F-39 *Do you collect diamonds* in the hope of striking it rich? (Turn to page 285.)

or

F-40 *Do you hold your funds in an asset management account* paying 8%, or $30,899, and wait for the right opportunity? (Turn to page 286.)

After you have made your decision, turn to the next page for the experts' comments.

THE EXPERTS STRATEGIZE:
F-39. DIAMONDS

Georgina Gold (Opportunistic Expert)—Commentary

The value of diamonds historically has grown at an annual rate that would be in excess of anything else you could invest in. Currently there is a great rush into investing in material objects as opposed to financial assets. The problem is you don't really know too much about diamonds and can't control the factors that affect their price. You lack the ability to price diamonds accurately. Over the long haul it is probably a good investment due to the DeBeers cartel. In the short term you could easily have a dip in the market.

F-40. ASSET MANAGEMENT
ACCOUNT

Jonathan Walker (Risk-Averse Expert)—Commentary

An asset management account is the most liquid income investment. You can deposit your money one day and take it out the next. The interest rate varies day by day with the general level of other rates in the economy. If rates go up, you get the immediate advantage of earning higher rates on your investment. However, if rates go down, your investment consequently will yield you less. Asset management accounts are very, very safe. The assets are comprised of CDs held at large domestic banks. These accounts are a great short-term holding place.

(Continued from page 125)

RESULTS:
E-21. SPREADSHEET $YSTEMS

THE EXPERTS SPEAK
Jonathan Walker

You win some and you lose some. After breaking the bank by investing in Spreadsheet $ystems and increasing your inheritance to over $500,000, you suffered from gambler's syndrome—you didn't know when to stop. You should have gotten out of Spreadsheet $ystems when the merger fell through. You had another chance to sell your shares when the company decided to diversify in the face of declining software sales and lowered profitability. In both cases you stayed on and as a result lost $200,000. Is there any question what you should do next?

Spreadsheet $ystems' diversification foray into computer hardware became unplugged. Response from the retail trade was at best lukewarm, although enthusiastic compared to consumer reaction. The problem was that the speech synthesizer sounded like an American speaking Japanese. In addition, cheaper units from more established companies recently came on the market, which completely undercut the newcomer. As a result, Spreadsheet $ystems' stock price fell 25%, meaning you lost $105,000. Your shares, once valued at $420,000, are now worth $315,000.

You're sick. If you stay with the company any longer, you'll be broke. In fact, you even heard that your ever-optimistic friend from the company was looking for a job. That's a bad sign. However, the latest management report from the company indicates that the firm may be acquired, which would send the stock price soaring. You figure a merger would be great, if there's anything left by the time it happens. You lost over $200,000 during the past two years. Maybe you should bail out now. On the other hand, maybe here's your chance to recoup your money.

You call up Leonard, your financial wizard, to ask for advice. If he were in your situation and had your track record of two losing years, he would put all the remaining money in either a blind trust or T bills. Safe, 8.2% T bills don't sound bad. You look over the numbers and consider how you want to invest your dwindling inheritance.

Bank Investment Advisory Newsletter

The economy continues to flex its muscle. The GNP grew 8% for the year. The index of leading economic indicators also gave the current administration something to cheer about, as the index grew a full 1%, led by the growth in the formation of new businesses and a dip in unemployment claims. Retail sales climbed above the monthly $100 billion level as Sears, J. C. Penney, and K Mart reported banner sales for the year. Inflation fell to 7%, while unemployment remained at 9%. New car sales are above the 10 million annual rate, while steel companies are showing some strength in cutting losses and fighting foreign competition. Corporate profits as a whole grew 13%, while the Dow Jones Industrial Averages set new records. At the same time the prime rate dropped another percent to 11% as rates across the board fell.

Government spending is under control, although conservatives and hawks condemn the recent lids on military spending, while liberals and social welfare advocates call the administration's reductions in the social welfare area unconscionable. Still, taxpayers who are paying less and consumers who are spending more are highly supportive . . .

SPREADSHEET $YSTEMS
CHAIRMAN'S MESSAGE TO SHAREHOLDERS

Despite the recent failure of the Speakeasy ™ speech synthesizer unit, Spreadsheet $ystems' management is bullish on the company. Sales of the company's computer software declined only slightly (10%), which was better than many other companies in the industry. Revenues from the software were $6.75 million, which meant losses were held to only $500,000 in this area. The loss attributable to the new speech synthesizer introduction was $1 million, although management still believes the unit is the best on the market. Total net loss for the year was $1.5 million.

The strength of our marketing and distribution should enable Spreadsheet $ystems to weather our current financial problems and return to profitability within a year. The company is currently engaged in merger discussions with a larger company, which prefers to remain anonymous . . .

DECISION F

The current value of your investment is *$315,000*. Tough luck, your investment is 5% below the average of the experts.

F-41 **Do you finally earn some money,** any money, **in 8.2% T bills** paying $25,830? (Turn to page 287.)

or

F-42 **Do you continue to roll the dice by keeping your Spreadsheet $ystems stock** and hope that it turns around or is acquired? (Turn to page 288.)

After you have made your decision, turn to the next page for the experts' comments.

THE EXPERTS STRATEGIZE:
F-41. T BILLS

Jonathan Walker (Risk-Averse Expert)—Commentary

T bills are absolutely the safest investment to put your money into. There is no risk on the principal. Your interest will be paid by the U.S. government. This is the place to put money when you don't really know what you want to do with it, yet you want to make sure you have it when you want it. Money can be withdrawn from T bills at any time. The markets are extremely liquid.

F-42. SPREADSHEET $YSTEMS

Chat Morton (High-Risk Expert)—Commentary

Things are getting worse. The net loss for the year was one and a half million dollars. The speech synthesizer introduction was a failure. Sales of video games are still declining. To stay with this company at this point is very risky. The promise of a merger is pie in the sky. It appears to be a desperation attempt by the company to keep the stock price up.

Your friend is a hazard to the investment community. He knows as little as or even less than most investment analysts. This company is going down fast, and you should not be in the stock.

(Continued from page 125)

RESULTS:
E-22. MUNICIPAL MUTUAL FUNDS

THE EXPERTS SPEAK
Georgina Gold

You got out in time by selling your Spreadsheet $ystems shares before the latest loss and made 11.5%. As a result, you managed to keep most of your newly earned principal intact. You still have almost a half million dollars. In the future, be careful before investing in a risky, struggling company. New companies as a matter of course are overly opportunistic, providing hope and visions of wealth for the greedy. Spreadsheet $ystems is losing money. Its products are failing in the marketplace. The industry is soft. Let your experience be a lesson, and don't let greed blind your vision. Most investors have enough trouble seeing clearly anyway.

You live and die with new companies. You finally decided that Spreadsheet $ystems, even with its new speech synthesizer, was a terminal case. You were right. The speech synthesizer adventure never panned out. Consumers never accepted the unit, which sounded even worse than the recorded messages you hear on Bell Telephone. Had you invested in Spreadsheet $ystems you would have lost 25% of your principal. Instead you invested in a tax-free municipal mutual fund, which earned 11.5%, or $48,300.

Mr. Theodore, your Yellow Pages discount broker who provides investment advice on the side, says you're a fool to consider anything other than munis. You have over $465,000 to invest. Why throw it away on a ne'er-do-well computer software company when you can earn $52,000 by keeping your money in safe munis?

You agree. You're all set to renew your munis when you glance at the latest report from Spreadsheet $ystems. It reports that progress is being made on the merger front. Stock prices have begun to climb in anticipation of Spreadsheet $ystems' being acquired. Your eyes light up like a computer game. You realize that a fool's worst enemy is himself or herself, but the thrill of going for broke (literally) is too much.

You try to calm yourself down as you weigh the excitement of Spreadsheet $ystems stock versus the guaranteed return offered by munis.

You look at the data, ponder, and decide.

Bank Investment Advisory Newsletter

The economy continues to flex its muscle. The GNP grew 8% for the year. The index of leading economic indicators also gave the current administration something to cheer about, as the index grew a full 1%, led by the growth in the formation of new businesses and a dip in unemployment claims. Retail sales climbed above the monthly $100 billion level as Sears, J. C. Penney, and K Mart reported banner sales for the year. Inflation fell to 7%, while unemployment remained at 9%. New car sales are above the 10 million annual rate, while steel companies are showing some strength in cutting losses and fighting foreign competition. Corporate profits as a whole grew 13%, while the Dow Jones Industrial Averages set new records. At the same time the prime rate dropped another percent to 11% as rates across the board fell.

Government spending is under control, although conservatives and hawks condemn the recent lids on military spending, while liberals and social welfare advocates call the administration's reductions in the social welfare area unconscionable. Still, taxpayers who are paying less and consumers who are spending more are highly supportive . . .

SPREADSHEET $YSTEMS
CHAIRMAN'S MESSAGE TO SHAREHOLDERS

Despite the recent failure of the Speakeasy ™ speech synthesizer unit, Spreadsheet $ystems' management is bullish on the company. Sales of the company's computer software declined only slightly (10%), which was better than many other companies in the industry. Revenues from the software were $6.75 million, which meant losses were held to only $500,000 in this area. The loss attributable to the new speech synthesizer introduction was $1 million, although management still believes the unit is the best on the market. Total net loss for the year was $1.5 million.

The strength of our marketing and distribution should enable Spreadsheet $ystems to weather our current financial problems and return to profitability within a year. The company is currently engaged in merger discussions with a larger company, which prefers to remain anonymous . . .

DECISION F

The current value of your investment is *$468,300*. Congratulations, your investment is 41% above the average of the experts.

F-43   **Do you keep your money in munis,** which pay a decent 11.2%, or $52,450? (Turn to page 287.)

or

F-44   **Do you gamble one last time to win and buy Spreadsheet $ystems shares?** (Turn to page 288.)

After you have made your decision, turn to the next page for the experts' choices.

THE EXPERTS STRATEGIZE:
F-43. MUNIS

Chat Morton (High-Risk Expert) did not take this alternative.

The munis provide a very decent rate of return, but they don't offer me any opportunity to expand my wealth. I have little more than quadrupled my investment, and the munis aren't going to help me on my path to fame and glory. There are rumors of a merger discussion. Spreadsheet $ystems stock prices have started to move up on that. What do I need a bond for? If I get lucky, I can make twice my money in Spreadsheet $ystems.

F-44. SPREADSHEET $YSTEMS

Chat Morton (High-Risk Expert) took this alternative.

An interesting situation has developed at Spreadsheet $ystems. While the company has tremendous problems, there is hope, since the management team still owns a good percentage of the company. I don't believe they are going to let themselves go down without a fight. I believe the opportunity for a merger is possible, and I want to partake. The old Chicago expression is very applicable here—Live fast, die young, and leave a good-looking corpse.

(Continued from page 130)

RESULTS:
E-23. PENNY STOCKS MUTUAL
FUND/MUNIS

THE EXPERTS SPEAK
———————— Georgina Gold ————————

Penny stocks are for nickel-and-dime investors, so when the companies go bankrupt the investors don't lose a lot of money. Penny stocks are pure risks. They are generally small new companies whose chances of success are between small and zero. Mining in California hasn't been profitable in years. There is a reason the big companies are not competing in this area, and it is not that they fear the competition of the newcomers. It is because of the difficulty in making money in wildcat mining operations. Don't blow your new-found wealth that you gambled so hard to earn on overly risky investments. You were lucky once with Spreadsheet Systems. Lightning rarely strikes twice on the same investor.

With penny stocks you can own controlling shares in a company. The only problem is that after a year there may be no company left to control. You invested in new mining and energy companies traded on the Denver Penny Stock Exchange. Unfortunately, none of the companies found anything in California, other than themselves. In addition, their future prospects look grim. Even the ever-reliable munis had some bad luck with repayments. As a result, your total investment decreased 35% in value, or over $208,000. If you don't act fast, you may even lose the rest.

Sell, sell, sell, you tell Mr. Theodore, the discount broker whose advice to buy the penny stocks was worth exactly what you paid for it. Mr. Theodore agrees. Now he recommends fixed-return municipals that pay 7% interest, equivalent to an 11.2% pre-tax return. Safe and conservative. You hesitate. You ask if there's anything between safe munis and disastrous penny stocks. Mr. Theodore hesitates. Then he responds, what about more speculative investments like power authority energy bonds? These are not nuclear issues but alternative-energy undertakings such as solar and hydroelectric projects. The bonds are rated higher than nuclear issues because disaster is more remote, yet the bonds have returned healthy yields in the past (between 8% and 14%).

Either investment doesn't sound bad. The question is, which sounds better? You look at the reports, scratch your head, and make a decision.

Bank Investment Advisory Newsletter

The economy continues to flex its muscle. The GNP grew 8% for the year. The index of leading economic indicators also gave the current administration something to cheer about, as the index grew a full 1%, led by the growth in the formation of new businesses and a dip in unemployment claims. Retail sales climbed above the monthly $100 billion level as Sears, J. C. Penney, and K Mart reported banner sales for the year. Inflation fell to 7%, while unemployment remained at 9%. New car sales are above the 10 million annual rate, while steel companies are showing some strength in cutting losses and fighting foreign competition. Corporate profits as a whole grew 13%, while the Dow Jones Industrial Averages set new records. At the same time the prime rate dropped another percent to 11% as rates across the board fell.

Government spending is under control, although conservatives and hawks condemn the recent lids on military spending, while liberals and social welfare advocates call the administration's reductions in the social welfare area unconscionable. Still, taxpayers who are paying less and consumers who are spending more are highly supportive . . .

POWER AUTHORITY BONDS
FREE INFORMATION FROM
THEODORE & ASSCC.

Not all power authorities across the country are building nuclear power plants. A growing number, especially on the West Coast, are constructing coal, hydroelectric, and solar facilities. Their returns are lower, but the risk is smaller when compared with nuclear issues. The latest bonds, all A-rated, include the Northwestern Sun Authority (11.5% return), the Mountain Stream Utility (13.4% return), and the Consolidated Energy Company (12% return). All have excellent track records and vast experience in building power plants. All are well capitalized and . . .

DECISION F

The current value of your investment is *$386,636*. Congratulations, your investment is 17% above the average of the experts.

F-45 **Do you stay conservative with 11.2% municipals,** paying $43,303 return on your investment? (Turn to page 287.)

or

F-46 **Do you invest in the power bonds to** give your investment a shot (either in the arm or the head)? (Turn to page 288.)

After you have made your decision, turn to the next page for the experts' comments.

THE EXPERTS STRATEGIZE: F-45. TAX-FREE MUNICIPALS

Jonathan Walker (Risk-Averse Expert)—Commentary

Why would anyone want to pay taxes? The 7% tax-free income is very good. The bonds are safe and can easily be bought and sold. The primary disadvantage is that if interest rates go up, the value of the bonds goes down. But in any case, the guaranteed pre-tax equivalent yield still is over 11%, year after year. A very safe and wise investment for the cautious at heart.

F-46. POWER AUTHORITY BONDS

Georgina Gold (Opportunistic Expert)—Commentary

Power authority bonds in general are safe investments as long as you avoid controversial ones like nuclear bonds. The power authorities are usually located in metropolitan areas, where there is a steady demand for power. Rate increases are generally granted on a regular basis by local rate-setting authorities, so earnings can be expected to grow steadily. This provides a lot of security for the bonds. These bonds have a good track record. They are all well capitalized. This seems to be a good, safe investment.

(Continued from page 130)

RESULTS:
E-24. NUCLEAR POWER AUTHORITY BOND FUND

THE EXPERTS SPEAK
Jonathan Walker

Successful nuclear issues are becoming like precious stones—rare finds. There are just too many potential problems with nuclear power plants, including cost overruns, licensing refusals, nuclear waste scares, and the like. The offered interest rate is irrelevant if the plants don't come online and the companies or power authorities go bankrupt. You did well in the past taking chances on Spreadsheet Systems. Why risk it all in the future? Use extreme caution when investing in investments like high-yielding energy bonds.

You wanted the safety of munis with a little speculative flair. Unfortunately, that flair cost you dearly. One of the power bonds in the fund you invested in developed severe problems. One of its nuclear power plants was denied licensing, even though the plant was 90% completed. While the plant still may be opened, it could take years. As a result, the company has temporarily suspended interest payments while it seeks additional financing. In the face of possible default and loss of interest, the bond decreased 50% in value, or more than $297,000. This is a real power failure.

Mr. Theodore, your normally unflappable investment advisor, says dump the bonds immediately and buy safe federal government notes paying 9%. While 9% isn't great, it sure beats heavy losses. If you want to speculate, he advises you to diversify your risk and invest in a Fortune 100 mutual fund. With an improving economy, the fund should do very well. You feel that even breaking even would be a small victory.

To speculate or not to speculate—that is the question. Maybe the numbers will help. If not, there is always prayer.

Bank Investment Advisory Newsletter

The economy continues to flex its muscle. The GNP grew 8% for the year. The index of leading economic indicators also gave the current administration something to cheer about, as the index grew a full 1%, led by the growth in the formation of new businesses and a dip in unemployment claims. Retail sales climbed above the monthly $100 billion level as Sears, J. C. Penney, and K Mart reported banner sales for the year. Inflation fell to 7%, while unemployment remained at 9%. New car sales are above the 10 million annual rate, while steel companies are showing some strength in cutting losses and fighting foreign competition. Corporate profits as a whole grew 13%, while the Dow Jones Industrial Averages set new records. At the same time the prime rate dropped another percent to 11% as rates across the board fell.

Government spending is under control, although conservatives and hawks condemn the recent lids on military spending, while liberals and social welfare advocates call the administration's reductions in the social welfare area unconscionable. Still, taxpayers who are paying less and consumers who are spending more are highly supportive . . .

T. KITZINGER'S MARKET OUTLOOK

The market has never been stronger. Trading is heavy with 100-million-share days no longer uncommon. The economy seems to be under control. Inflation is in check, while even interest rates have declined. The Dow Jones Averages have rallied in the past three months. The Standard and Poor's 500 gained 10 points over the last quarter. A composite index shows losers are now a small . . . For the next six to nine months, economists at the major brokerage houses are predicting continued strong performance with some big winners and very few losers. Institutional buying continues to be heavy, especially in blue-chip and energy issues. Attractive stocks to watch are . . .

DECISION F

The current value of your investment is $297,413. Tough luck, your investment is 10% below the average of the experts.

F-47   ***Do you*** go for absolute security and ***buy 9% government notes*** yielding a modest $26,767? (Turn to page 287.)

or

F-48   ***Do you play the market with a Fortune 100 index*** as it goes up (and down)? (Turn to page 288.)

After you have made your decision, turn to the next page for the experts' comments.

THE EXPERTS STRATEGIZE: F-47. GOVERNMENT NOTES

Jonathan Walker (Risk-Averse Expert)—Commentary

Government notes are like government Treasury bills except they take a little bit longer to mature. They typically mature in about five to ten years, although they can be sold at any time. They're very liquid and extremely safe. They pay a little bit more interest than the government T bills, so your income is slightly higher. A solid, risk-free investment.

F-48. FORTUNE 100 INDEX FUND

Georgina Gold (Opportunistic Expert)—Commentary

An index fund is an inexpensive way to buy into the broad movements of the market. If you wanted to buy each stock in the index individually, you would have to purchase approximately 100 different stocks. By buying a share in the fund, you avoid incurring additional costs and trouble.

This looks like it would be an excellent investment. The economy is good, government spending is under control, and the stock market has never been stronger. Institutional buying is very heavy, with prices going up. All the economic statistics are pointing to higher prices. A Fortune 100 index, by giving you access to 100 stocks, will make sure that you participate in an upward move in the market.

(Continued from page 134)

RESULTS:
E-25. HOLLYWOOD/MOVIES

THE EXPERTS SPEAK
Chat Morton

After three years of slow, plodding financial growth, you had a vision of making money in movies. You should have let the vision pass. Hollywood is a tough investment game. Success depends on the fickle tastes of the American consuming public, which no one has been able to figure out completely. Only the sale of subsidiary rights has removed some of the risk. It is difficult to get rich quick, as many bankrupt Hollywood investors can testify to. The real decision you must make is to pick your life-style and then choose an investment strategy accordingly.

Metro-Goldwyn-Mayer and you. Movie moguls. Riches beyond belief. The hopes and dreams that Hollywood is made of. Unfortunately, as investments, movies rank right up there with new car companies and new football leagues in terms of risk. You might as well go to Las Vegas and play the crap tables. The odds are better, and at least you might enjoy yourself in the process.

The movie you invested in returned only 10¢ on the dollar, although the auxiliary rights (i.e., cable, foreign distribution, T-shirts, and so forth) raised the total return to 80¢ on the dollar. Hence, you lost only $58,158 on the deal. Hollywood insiders consider you lucky.

You definitely will not invest in movies again, so Leonard suggests Broadway. The shows are cheaper to produce and slightly less risky because shows are easier to revise if they bomb. If you've got taste and can spot a winner, Leonard knows just the show. It's a light comedy on the life of Martin Luther. It has universal appeal. You don't think the show has a prayer, although the script is funny. Leonard says you could invest in 10% corporate bonds if you don't want a glamorous life-style.

Tough choice. Should you or should you not throw out your money on a Broadway show. Numbers wouldn't help.

Bank Investment Advisory Newsletter

The economy continues to flex its muscle. The GNP grew 8% for the year. The index of leading economic indicators also gave the current administration something to cheer about, as the index grew a full 1%, led by the growth in the formation of new businesses and a dip in unemployment claims. Retail sales climbed above the monthly $100 billion level as Sears, J. C. Penney, and K Mart reported banner sales for the year. Inflation fell to 7%, while unemployment remained at 9%. New car sales are above the 10 million annual rate, while steel companies are showing some strength in cutting losses and fighting foreign competition. Corporate profits as a whole grew 13%, while the Dow Jones Industrial Averages set new records. At the same time the prime rate dropped another percent to 11% as rates across the board fell.

Government spending is under control, although conservatives and hawks condemn the recent lids on military spending, while liberals and social welfare advocates call the administration's reductions in the social welfare area unconscionable. Still, taxpayers who are paying less and consumers who are spending more are highly supportive . . .

Not a Prayer—A PROPOSAL

The lighter side of Martin Luther provides the backdrop for this light comedy. Set in medieval Europe of the 1500s, this three-person show follows Luther as he tactfully tries to reform the church. Negotiations are already underway for casting. The show is budgeted at $1 million. Shares are being sold in $10,000 units. The writer is Terry Geoff, whose list of credits include *The Nun's Bad Habit* and *Kosher Pork.* The producers also have a successful track record with such hits as . . .

DECISION F

The current value of your investment is *$232,631.* Tough luck, your investment is 30% below the average of the experts.

F-49 **Do you risk breaking a leg (or your neck) by investing in a Broadway comedy on Martin Luther?** (Turn to page 287.)

or

F-50 **Do you buy a 10% corporate bond** returning a dignified $23,263? (Turn to page 288.)

After you have made your decision, turn to the next page for the experts' comments.

THE EXPERTS STRATEGIZE:
F-49. BROADWAY

Georgina Gold (Opportunistic Expert)—Commentary

Investing in Broadway plays doesn't make sense. The idea of a comedy on Martin Luther, who is reputed to be a little funnier than Calvin Coolidge, is an even worse idea. You don't know anything about this play; to invest in it is the same as giving it away.

F-50. CORPORATE BONDS

Jonathan Walker (Risk-Averse Expert)—Commentary

Corporate bonds typically are very safe. They are debt with a senior claim on a company's assets if the company develops any problems. The 10% interest is good. The only risk is if interest rates go up sharply, then the price of the bonds will drop. It is possible to reduce this risk by buying shorter term bonds.

The economy seems to favor an investment of this type. Inflation is falling, which should help interest rates. As a result, in the near term there should be little principal risk. In addition, the bonds provide a decent return from interest.

(Continued from page 134)

RESULTS:
E-26. TIME DEPOSITS

THE EXPERTS SPEAK
——————————— Chat Morton ———————————

Strategically you have chosen a conservative course. After making $100,000 on the new computer software company in one year, you have picked risk-free investments that will take you four years to make that amount again. Does this strategy make sense in a growing economy? Financially, no. Psychologically, maybe. There are always opportunities out there when the GNP is up, interest rates are down, and industry is healthy. On the other hand, you may prefer the security of seeing steady growth in your investment principal. Only you can decide.

———————————————————————————————

Continuing to buy time deposits is like going to a Baskin-Robbins and ordering vanilla. Sure it's good, but there are so many other choices available. Still, you have made 10% or more for the fourth consecutive year. Your investment increased by $29,000 to a hefty $320,000.

Taxes are beginning to worry you. After all, you're rich—or almost rich. Leonard, your advisor, suggests tax-free municipals, which are relatively safe investments with good yields. They're currently paying 11.2% (pre-tax equivalent). What if you want to live a little more dangerously, you ask? Leonard says then you should try a speculative mutual fund specializing in energy issues. The fund buys companies with interests in all forms of energy, including oil, gas, nuclear, solar, and so on. This diversification cuts down the risk in a risky business.

Still you're uncertain. You made almost $60,000 in the last two years, which isn't too bad. By not speculating, you're winning, but not by a wide margin. How much is enough? You remember the investment adage, bears and bulls win, but pigs never do.

You sit down and review the data before you decide.

Bank Investment Advisory Newsletter

The economy continues to flex its muscle. The GNP grew 8% for the year. The index of leading economic indicators also gave the current administration something to cheer about, as the index grew a full 1%, led by the growth in the formation of new businesses and a dip in unemployment claims. Retail sales climbed above the monthly $100 billion level as Sears, J. C. Penney, and K Mart reported banner sales for the year. Inflation fell to 7%, while unemployment remained at 9%. New car sales are above the 10 million annual rate, while steel companies are showing some strength in cutting losses and fighting foreign competition. Corporate profits as a whole grew 13%, while the Dow Jones Industrial Averages set new records. At the same time the prime rate dropped another percent to 11% as rates across the board fell.

Government spending is under control, although conservatives and hawks condemn the recent lids on military spending, while liberals and social welfare advocates call the administration's reductions in the social welfare area unconscionable. Still, taxpayers who are paying less and consumers who are spending more are highly supportive . . .

MERIT-PYNCH INVESTMENT REPORT

MUTUAL FUNDS— ENERGY FIELD

The cost of finding and producing energy has risen dramatically in the past ten years. Ever since the energy crisis of the early 1970s, there has been concern that energy supplies will dwindle in the coming decades. Despite occasional temporary gluts in certain energy markets, such as oil, the basic underlying shortage remains. The EnergAll Mutual Fund is a specialized fund which invests in companies involved in energy exploration, production, and distribution. The fund has done exceedingly well in the past, with average gains of 18%+ for the last four years. The fund's current portfolio includes two major oil companies, three natural gas distributors, two uranium mining companies . . .

DECISION F

The current value of your investment is *$319,868*. Tough luck, your investment is 3% below the average of the experts.

F-51 **Do you avoid taxes and buy the municipals** yielding 11.2%, or $35,825? (Turn to page 289.)

or

F-52 **Do you** throw caution to the winds and **speculate in a mutual fund specializing in energy issues?** (Turn to page 290.)

After you have made your decision, turn to the next page for the experts' comments.

THE EXPERTS STRATEGIZE: F-51. TAX-FREE MUNICIPALS

Jonathan Walker (Risk-Averse Expert)—Commentary

Why would anyone want to pay taxes? The 7% tax-free income is very good. The bonds are safe and can easily be bought and sold. The primary disadvantage is that if interest rates go up, the value of the bonds goes down. But in any case, the guaranteed pre-tax equivalent yield still is over 11%, year after year. A very safe and wise investment for the cautious at heart.

F-52. ENERGY MUTUAL FUND

Georgina Gold (Opportunistic Expert)—Commentary

The advantages of an energy mutual fund are professional management and a large amount of diversification in the energy field. Some of these investments can be quite conservative, such as in oil companies with large assets and earnings. On the other hand, other investments in the fund can be risky, such as in companies that are small and speculative, whose future prospects might depend on a number of successful projects. So over the long term this fund might provide some interesting returns because energy always will be needed. Over the short term, it is risky.

(Continued from page 139)

RESULTS:
E-27. CERTIFICATES OF DEPOSIT

THE EXPERTS SPEAK
Chat Morton

Back to home base. After investing in a high-flier fund which yielded only 3%, you decided to return to safe, risk-free investments like CDs. The strategy is not bad in that you will never (or hardly ever) lose money in safe investments. However, it's impossible to make a lot of money that way, too. The economy is on the move with the index of leading economic indicators up. Consumer spending is up. The prime rate is down. Now is the time to take advantage of these favorable economic signs. Don't wait.

Anybody can make money on CDs—even you. The CDs did not let you down. You made a full 11% on your investment, or almost $30,000. That's great as long as you continue to work and never plan to retire. You feel like you need a big hit, and you're not going to get it on fixed-return investments paying 11%. You need high double-digit increases—the kind that are sometimes found in inflation and taxes.

You tell yourself now is the time to act and call Leonard. He says you can make a fortune if you can only guess which way stock prices are going. If you can guess correctly, then you should buy options. Besides, he knows just the options for you—a mining company that is on the verge of major gold discoveries. It's risky—but you could strike it rich. It also could turn out to be the pits. If you want something less risky, then Leonard says you should buy a 10% corporate bond returning $30,000, but then you'll be no better off than you were before.

You're indecisive. You look at the data, search for inspiration, and then guess.

Bank Investment Advisory Newsletter

The economy continues to flex its muscle. The GNP grew 8% for the year. The index of leading economic indicators also gave the current administration something to cheer about, as the index grew a full 1%, led by the growth in the formation of new businesses and a dip in unemployment claims. Retail sales climbed above the monthly $100 billion level as Sears, J. C. Penney, and K Mart reported banner sales for the year. Inflation fell to 7%, while unemployment remained at 9%. New car sales are above the 10 million annual rate, while steel companies are showing some strength in cutting losses and fighting foreign competition. Corporate profits as a whole grew 13%, while the Dow Jones Industrial Averages set new records. At the same time the prime rate dropped another percent to 11% as rates across the board fell.

Government spending is under control, although conservatives and hawks condemn the recent lids on military spending, while liberals and social welfare advocates call the administration's reductions in the social welfare area unconscionable. Still, taxpayers who are paying less and consumers who are spending more are highly supportive . . .

PRECIOUS METTLE □□□
An investment analysis□□

THE OUTLOOK FOR GOLD

The low price of gold continues to confound analysts. Gold was expected to rise after apparently bottoming out in the early '80s. Given world instability and the need for financial security, predictions were made that gold would increase a minimum of 30% in value during the past year. This has not happened. In addition, the supply of gold has not expanded as much as had been forecast last year. The effect of the bank debt abroad is uncertain. Analysts are divided on the future of gold and its value as an investment . . .

DECISION F

The current value of your investment is $299,512. Tough luck, your investment is 10% below the average of the experts.

F-53 *Do you buy stock options of a gold mining company* that could or could not pan out? (Turn to page 289.)

or

F-54 *Do you invest in safe, 10% corporate bonds,* which return a guaranteed $29,951 regardless of what happens? (Turn to page 290.)

After you have made your decision, turn to the next page for the experts' comments.

THE EXPERTS STRATEGIZE: F-53. GOLD MINING STOCK OPTIONS

Chat Morton (High-Risk Expert)—Commentary

This choice is total speculation. Options on gold mining company stocks combine two extremely risky elements: the mining companies themselves and options as investment instruments. Gold mining company fortunes vary directly with the price of gold, which itself is quite erratic. Nobody has been able successfully to predict the price of gold for any length of time, since it is controlled by the South African government and other unstable political forces around the world. Options also are unpredictable, thus compounding the amount of risk. This would be one investment to avoid at all costs.

F-54. CORPORATE BONDS

Jonathan Walker (Risk-Averse Expert)—Commentary

Corporate bonds typically are very safe. They are debt with a senior claim on a company's assets if the company develops any problems. The 10% interest is good. The only risk is if interest rates go up sharply, then the price of the bonds will drop. It is possible to reduce this risk by buying shorter term bonds.

The economy seems to favor an investment of this type. Inflation is falling, which should help interest rates. As a result, in the near term there should be little principal risk. In addition, the bonds provide a decent return from interest.

(Continued from page 139)

RESULTS:
E-28. SPREADSHEET $YSTEMS

THE EXPERTS SPEAK
Chat Morton

High tech may appeal to you, but high finance obviously doesn't. After investing in a high-tech fund which returned only 3%, you put your money into a high-tech company with declining sales, decreasing profitability, and dubious new products. It's no wonder that you lost 25% of your money in Spreadsheet $ystems. Investors favor high tech because they think every new venture will be the next IBM, Apple, or Xerox. Most high-tech firms lose money and remain unknown for good reason. Separating the winners from the losers is very difficult to do.

You figured if you lost money on a high-flier mutual fund, why not really speculate and buy up Spreadsheet $ystems shares? You thought the shift of direction to computer hardware couldn't go wrong. After all, computers are the latest consumer rage. Unfortunately, Spreadsheet $ystems was not an active participant in this rage. Its speech synthesizer unit bombed, and its stock price took a nosedive. Your investment is now worth only 75% of what it previously was worth. In plain English, you lost $67,000.

You tell Leonard to sell your Spreadsheet $ystems shares and buy anything but a computer software company. Leonard says not so fast. He has heard that a big company is considering buying up Spreadsheet $ystems. That would send the price of the stock upward. Besides, if you keep your Spreadsheet $ystems shares, you can't lose much more, because the stock can't go much lower without the company going out of business. Very comforting, you think. You inquire, is there anything else to invest in? Leonard says that for complete safety there are government T bills. At least the government won't go out of business—at least not for a year, anyway.

You think about the risk/return tradeoff (whatever that is), look at the reports, and make a decision.

Bank Investment Advisory Newsletter

The economy continues to flex its muscle. The GNP grew 8% for the year. The index of leading economic indicators also gave the current administration something to cheer about, as the index grew a full 1%, led by the growth in the formation of new businesses and a dip in unemployment claims. Retail sales climbed above the monthly $100 billion level as Sears, J. C. Penney, and K Mart reported banner sales for the year. Inflation fell to 7%, while unemployment remained at 9%. New car sales are above the 10 million annual rate, while steel companies are showing some strength in cutting losses and fighting foreign competition. Corporate profits as a whole grew 13%, while the Dow Jones Industrial Averages set new records. At the same time the prime rate dropped another percent to 11% as rates across the board fell.

Government spending is under control, although conservatives and hawks condemn the recent lids on military spending, while liberals and social welfare advocates call the administration's reductions in the social welfare area unconscionable. Still, taxpayers who are paying less and consumers who are spending more are highly supportive . . .

SPREADSHEET $YSTEMS
CHAIRMAN'S MESSAGE TO SHAREHOLDERS

Despite the recent failure of the Speakeasy ™ speech synthesizer unit, Spreadsheet $ystems' management is bullish on the company. Sales of the company's computer software declined only slightly (10%), which was better than many other companies in the industry. Revenues from the software were $6.75 million, which meant losses were held to only $500,000 in this area. The loss attributable to the new speech synthesizer introduction was $1 million, although management still believes the unit is the best on the market. Total net loss for the year was $1.5 million.

The strength of our marketing and distribution should enable Spreadsheet $ystems to weather our current financial problems and return to profitability within a year. The company is currently engaged in merger discussions with a larger company, which prefers to remain anonymous . . .

DECISION F

The current value of your investment is *$202,373*. Tough luck, your investment is 39% below the average of the experts.

F-55 **Do you keep your Spreadsheet $ystems stock,** hoping there is some underlying value in the company? (Turn to page 289.)

or

F-56 **Do you sell your Spreadsheet $ystems shares** before you lose another 25% **and buy 8.2% T bills** yielding $16,595? (Turn to page 290.)

After you have made your decision, turn to the next page for the experts' comments.

THE EXPERTS STRATEGIZE:
F-55. SPREADSHEET $YSTEMS

Chat Morton (High-Risk Expert)—Commentary
  Things are getting worse. The net loss for the year was one
and a half million dollars. The speech synthesizer introduction was a failure. Sales of financial programs are still declining. To stay with this company at this point is very risky.
The promise of a merger is pie in the sky and appears to be
a desperation attempt by the company to keep the stock price
up. The company is failing. So watch out.

F-56. T BILLS

Jonathan Walker (Risk-Averse Expert)—Commentary
  T bills are absolutely the safest investment to put your
money into. There is no risk on the principal. Your interest
will be paid by the U.S. government. This is the place to put
money when you don't really know what you want to do with
it, yet you want to make sure you have it when you want it.
Money can be withdrawn from T bills at any time. The markets are extremely liquid.

(Continued from page 144)

RESULTS:
E-29. CONVERTIBLE DEBENTURES

THE EXPERTS SPEAK
—————————— Jonathan Walker ——————————

You're finally back on track after a 25% loss in grain commodities and a measly 10% gain with a corporate bond. The
American Diversified Industries convertible bond yielded a

healthy 15%, because basically the company is good and the economy is growing. Given these circumstances, convertible bonds are the right investment. All the economic signs continue to point upward. Stay with value and growth, and you can't go too far wrong.

You wanted the sure 8% and you got it. Plus the value of the bond increased 7% as the price of the stock skyrocketed. Your total gain was a whopping 15%, or $28,000. You also reviewed the Dow Jones Futures that you didn't choose and noticed their value had declined 13%. Lucky you. Do wonders never cease? You made the right choice and actually made money.

Leonard advises you to hold the American Diversified Industries bond at this time because the company stock can only go up. You wonder, up like hot air and taxes? Still, the company has great products and a great track record. You're only concerned that the stock may have peaked. Even if sales and revenues continue to grow, unless Wall Street analysts are satisfied, the market may not support higher prices for the stock. If you feel that way, Leonard says, then why not buy a 9 1/2% corporate bond. It's safe yet still a full point and a half above the guaranteed return of the convertible bond.

You're in a quandry. In the past you were able to get both safety and growth when you bought convertible bonds. Now you can have either growth with stocks or safety with the corporate bonds. It's decision time as you review all the data.

Bank Investment Advisory Newsletter

The economy continues to flex its muscle. The GNP grew 8% for the year. The index of leading economic indicators also gave the current administration something to cheer about, as the index grew a full 1%, led by the growth in the formation of new businesses and a dip in unemployment claims. Retail sales climbed above the monthly $100 billion level as Sears, J. C. Penney, and K Mart reported banner sales for the year. Inflation fell to 7%, while unemployment remained at 9%. New car sales are above the 10 million annual rate, while steel companies are showing some strength in cutting losses and fighting foreign competition. Corporate profits as a whole grew 13%, while the Dow Jones Industrial Averages set new records. At the same time the prime rate dropped another percent to 11% as rates across the board fell.

Government spending is under control, although conservatives and hawks condemn the recent lids on military spending, while liberals and social welfare advocates call the administration's reductions in the social welfare area unconscionable. Still, taxpayers who are paying less and consumers who are spending more are highly supportive . . .

Street Scene Magazine

"CONGLOMERATES CAN WORK"

American Diversified Industries' fast food and financial operations continue to grow at a breakneck pace. Both experienced growth in revenue and sales of 30% +. If the rather staid, conservative fashion line had kept pace, the company would have reported an even larger profit. Sales topped $800 million, while net income rose to $65 million.

The fast food operation is thinking of expanding into the Southwest, and its management has already acquired 10 prime locations in Texas. The financial services division has bought an investment advisory house, which means the company can offer complete investment services. The only note of caution is a question as to how long this great growth can continue . . . This house recommends the stock as a "buy" for the short term . . .

DECISION F

The current value of your investment is *$218,023*. Tough luck, your investment is 34% below the average of the experts.

F-57   **Do you hold the bonds** and hope the stock is as good as you think it is? (turn to page 289.)

or

F-58   **Do you** believe the best investment is the safest one and **invest in 9.5% corporate bonds** yielding $20,712? (Turn to page 290.)

After you have made your decision, turn to the next page for the experts' comments.

THE EXPERTS STRATEGIZE: F-57. CONVERTIBLE BONDS

Georgina Gold (Opportunistic Expert)—Commentary

This convertible bond continues to be an attractive issue. With a guaranteed 8% yield and a rising stock price, it continues to be a wise choice. American Diversified Industries' businesses are growing. Sales and profits are up. Brokerage houses recommend it for the short term. You might as well stick with success.

F-58. CORPORATE BONDS

Jonathan Walker (Risk-Averse Expert)—Commentary

Corporate bonds typically are very safe. They are debt with a senior claim on a company's assets if the company develops any problems. The 9.5% interest is good. The only risk is if interest rates go up sharply, then the price of the bonds will drop. It is possible to reduce this risk by buying shorter term bonds.

The economy seems to favor an investment of this type. Inflation is falling, which should help interest rates. As a result, in the near term there should be little principal risk. In addition, the bonds provide a decent return from interest.

(Continued from page 144)

RESULTS:
E-30. DOW JONES FUTURES

THE EXPERTS SPEAK
———————— Jonathan Walker ————————

Who would have ever guessed that in a healthy, growing economy you could lose money? You can do it with futures. Futures investing in stock market averages requires that you guess not only which way the market is going, but also how far. You came up short. Unless you are at least 75% certain of your market predictions (and no one really ever is), try another investment and leave futures to professional brokers who gamble with other people's money.

Futures is a tough game, like boxing. After a few rounds, you've either won or you need your head examined. Unfortunately, you need your head examined. You lost—not because you didn't guess correctly that the Dow Jones Averages would go up (they go up about two thirds of the time anyway), but because the rate of increase was too small for you to make any money. Hence, you lost 13%, or $25,000, on your $190,000 investment. Oh well, there's always tomorrow for futures.

Leonard says stick it out. Hold on to the futures. They'll pay off in the long run. The economy continues to improve, and stocks will only do better—a lot better. Sure, you could make 10% in time deposits, but what's a paltry 10%, or $16,500? After losing $25,000 on futures, you think a 10% gain would be great. Still, Leonard does have a point. Since you buy futures with only a small down payment, you can make a lot of money quickly (assuming of course the Dow Jones Averages go up). If they start to fall, you can protect your downside risk by issuing a sell price, at which point the futures are automatically sold. What could be better?

You review the monthly economic newsletter, think, and decide.

Bank Investment Advisory Newsletter

The economy continues to flex its muscle. The GNP grew 8% for the year. The index of leading economic indicators also gave the current administration something to cheer about, as the index grew a full 1%, led by the growth in the formation of new businesses and a dip in unemployment claims. Retail sales climbed above the monthly $100 billion level as Sears, J. C. Penney, and K Mart reported banner sales for the year. Inflation fell to 7%, while unemployment remained at 9%. New car sales are above the 10 million annual rate, while steel companies are showing some strength in cutting losses and fighting foreign competition. Corporate profits as a whole grew 13%, while the Dow Jones Industrial Averages set new records. At the same time the prime rate dropped another percent to 11% as rates across the board fell.

Government spending is under control, although conservatives and hawks condemn the recent lids on military spending, while liberals and social welfare advocates call the administration's reductions in the social welfare area unconscionable. Still, taxpayers who are paying less and consumers who are spending more are highly supportive . . .

T. KITZINGER'S
MARKET OUTLOOK

The market has never been stronger. Trading is heavy with 100-million-share days no longer uncommon. The economy seems to be under control. Inflation is in check, while even interest rates have declined. The Dow Jones Averages have rallied in the past three months. The Standard and Poor's 500 gained 10 points over the last quarter. A composite index shows losers are now a small . . . For the next six to nine months, economists at the major brokerage houses are predicting continued strong performance with some big winners and very few losers. Institutional buying continues to be heavy, especially in blue-chip and energy issues. Attractive stocks to watch are . . .

DECISION F

The current value of your investment is *$164,939*. Tough luck, your investment is 50% below the average of the experts.

F-59   **Do you continue** to try your luck **in the risky market futures game,** which has a lot of margin for error? (Turn to page 289.)

or

F-60   **Do you** believe "neither a borrower nor a loser be" and **buy safe, 10% time deposits** returning $16,494? (Turn to page 290.)

After you have made your decision, turn to the next page for the experts' comments.

THE EXPERTS STRATEGIZE:
F-59. DOW JONES FUTURES

Georgina Gold (Opportunistic Expert)—Commentary

Futures are an extremely risky investment. They are even riskier than options, since you are never exactly sure what your total losses might be. If the index appreciates sharply past the strike price or break-even point, the value of your futures will go up accordingly. If the index goes down, you could take a very large loss.

At this point it looks like Dow Jones Futures might be a safe bet, but you are going to need a very strong stomach. The market has never been stronger. The economy is extremely robust, and all the economic indices are doing better. Institutions are realizing this and have been buying stocks very heavily. It's a good bet stock prices will continue to go up, and therefore futures could be very profitable.

F-60. TIME DEPOSITS

Jonathan Walker (Risk-Averse Expert)—Commentary

Time deposits are among the safest investments you can make. They are typically for very short periods of time, ranging from one week to several years. You get a fixed return and your investment is guaranteed up to $100,000 by the FDIC. The one unattractive feature of time deposits is that they are not marketable, meaning you must pay a penalty if you withdraw your money before they mature. But in general they are good, sound investments.

(Continued from page 148)

RESULTS:
E-31. CERTIFICATES OF DEPOSIT

THE EXPERTS SPEAK
Jonathan Walker

After losing $100,000 on grain and gold, making money—even $12,000—is a new and pleasant experience. Commodities, whether they be grain or gold, are always risky. Even when you diversify the risk through buying a commodities index, you still are taking a chance. Despite the fact that you passed over diamonds which did well, it is still true that you should invest in commodities only if you enjoy speculating, not for the purpose of making money. Speculating oftentimes is an end in and of itself.

You avoided temptation and invested in safe, 10% CDs only to find out that diamonds are forever—or at the very least for a year. While you made a meager 10%, or $12,000, fashionable diamonds climbed a full 25%. While 10% isn't bad, you fell like the best man at a wedding—you're the best man in name only.

Maybe now is the time to get back into commodities. But the question is, how do you avoid the beating you took in grain and gold? You call up Leonard. He thinks for thirty seconds (which is a long time for any financial expert) and suggests a commodities index. The index is made up of the top twelve commodities: grain, wheat, corn, pork bellies, gold, and so forth. Even if a couple of the commodities bomb out, the average should do well. The index itself is new, but had there been such an index in the past, it would have gained an average of 25% per year. That's way above the Dow Jones and other stock market averages. Besides, the index is well managed and professionals recommend it. (You wonder whether they actually buy it.) Leonard says it sure beats the safe alternative—9.5% CDs. You only hope he is right.

Commodities or CDs? You look at the reports and make a choice.

Bank Investment Advisory Newsletter

The economy continues to flex its muscle. The GNP grew 8% for the year. The index of leading economic indicators also gave the current administration something to cheer about, as the index grew a full 1%, led by the growth in the formation of new businesses and a dip in unemployment claims. Retail sales climbed above the monthly $100 billion level as Sears, J. C. Penney, and K Mart reported banner sales for the year. Inflation fell to 7%, while unemployment remained at 9%. New car sales are above the 10 million annual rate, while steel companies are showing some strength in cutting losses and fighting foreign competition. Corporate profits as a whole grew 13%, while the Dow Jones Industrial Averages set new records. At the same time the prime rate dropped another percent to 11% as rates across the board fell.

Government spending is under control, although conservatives and hawks condemn the recent lids on military spending, while liberals and social welfare advocates call the administration's reductions in the social welfare area unconscionable. Still, taxpayers who are paying less and consumers who are spending more are highly supportive . . .

■STAPLE ITEMS■
A REPORT ON COMMODITIES

As all investors know, even beginners, the commodity market is highly volatile. Fortunes can be made and lost in days—or even in hours. To counter some of this volatility yet still take advantage of the money that can be made in commodities, an index of the top twelve commodities has been put together for investors. The top twelve commodities include copper, gold, wheat, corn, oil . . . The outlook for each commodity is listed below. Wheat: The market is strong, while the supply is limited. Acreage reduction programs and a major drought have reduced supply, while foreign demand has increased . . . Gold: The price of this precious metal has remained in the doldrums. After the price fell below $400 an ounce, analysts expected it to rebound in the face of world instability, which in the past had set off a surge in gold purchases. This year demand has remained low . . . Oil: The supply of oil is . . .

DECISION F

The current value of your investment is *$134,585*. Tough luck, your investment is 59% below the average of the experts.

F-61 **Do you put your money into the top twelve commodities index** and hope to make a killing, just like the professionals? (Turn to page 291.)

or

F-62 **Do you bank your money in safe, 9.5% CDs** paying $12,786? (Turn to page 292.)

After you have made your decision, turn to the next page for the experts' comments.

THE EXPERTS STRATEGIZE:
F-61. TOP TWELVE COMMODITIES

Georgina Gold (Opportunistic Expert)—Commentary

An investment in this type of index is generally chosen with the aid of a trend-tracking mechanism. The person who invests your money will draw graphs of the various price movements in the different underlying commodities and try to spot long-term trend formations. This strategy is not fool-proof and really doesn't have any basis in logic. Yet it seems to work. Believe it or not, this type of fund has been relatively successful. This investment though, is a calculated risk.

F-62. CERTIFICATES OF DEPOSIT

Jonathan Walker (Risk-Averse Expert)—Commentary

CDs are a solid investment. They are monies which are used by large banks and other financial institutions to help fund their normal lending operations. They provide plenty of security and a low but guaranteed yield. They also are in-sured up to $100,000 by the federal government. As an investor, you should ask yourself whether you want or need a safe, risk-free investment. The answer to this question will determine whether or not you choose CDs.

(Continued from page 148)

RESULTS:
E-32. DIAMONDS

THE EXPERTS SPEAK
Chat Morton

Redemption. You have proven your investment expertise by making $30,000 in diamonds after losing heavily in grain and gold. You also were lucky. Diamonds are the same type of investment as gold and therefore are considered risky and unpredictable. Maybe that's what makes them attractive to investors. It is unclear whether diamonds will continue to rise, so you might want to take heed of the diamond analysts who urge caution in buying diamonds for investments.

All that glitters is not gold. After losing money on gold stocks, you decided to try diamonds. Diamonds did brilliantly. World instability, cutbacks in production, and new fashion trends have combined to produce a 25%, or $31,000, increase in your principal. Your investment is now worth $153,000.

Leonard calls to advise you to liquidate your position in diamonds immediately and buy T bills. Rumors of a major sell-off by the Soviet Union could send diamond prices tumbling. You ask, what if the Russians don't sell off their diamonds? Then you have made a fortune, Leonard replies. However, it's risky to wait it out. Better to buy T bills, he warns. The T bills pay 8.2%, or over $12,000, guaranteed.

Blinded by your new-found wealth, you're inclined to keep the diamonds. After all, you made the other decisions and you're wealthy. Besides, if you're wrong and you lose all your money, you could always become a financial advisor and make money advising other people.

Now is the time to act. The real issue is whether over the long run you see yourself buying diamonds or T bills. As you read the reports, you know they will only confirm the decision you have already made.

Bank Investment Advisory Newsletter

The economy continues to flex its muscle. The GNP grew 8% for the year. The index of leading economic indicators also gave the current administration something to cheer about, as the index grew a full 1%, led by the growth in the formation of new businesses and a dip in unemployment claims. Retail sales climbed above the monthly $100 billion level as Sears, J. C. Penney, and K Mart reported banner sales for the year. Inflation fell to 7%, while unemployment remained at 9%. New car sales are above the 10 million annual rate, while steel companies are showing some strength in cutting losses and fighting foreign competition. Corporate profits as a whole grew 13%, while the Dow Jones Industrial Averages set new records. At the same time the prime rate dropped another percent to 11% as rates across the board fell.

Government spending is under control, although conservatives and hawks condemn the recent lids on military spending, while liberals and social welfare advocates call the administration's reductions in the social welfare area unconscionable. Still, taxpayers who are paying less and consumers who are spending more are highly supportive . . .

PRECIOUS METTLE □ □□ □
An investment analysis□ □

DIAMONDS—INVESTMENT OUTLOOK

Prices recently skyrocketed, brought on by increased demand and curtailed production, but many analysts are urging caution for fear the price structure may fall. Some price erosion was noted in the third quarter, although the fourth quarter of the year was particularly strong. World production increased by 25% and is expected to remain at a higher level for the foreseeable future. Prices could drop if the Russians sell off large quantities to finance military adventures. As a result, most analysts advise a "hold" policy, while a few urge liquidation for the long term and are "neutral" for the short term . . . Two prominent analysts, however, advocate increased holdings as a means . . .

DECISION F

The current value of your investment is $152,938. Tough luck, your investment is 54% below the average of the experts.

F-63 **Do you buy 8.2% government T bills** yielding $12,541 to maintain the safety and security of your middle class existence? (Turn to page 291.)

or

F-64 **Do you keep your diamonds** in hopes of living better in the future? (Turn to page 292.)

After you have made your decision, turn to the next page for the experts' comments.

THE EXPERTS STRATEGIZE: F-63. T BILLS

Jonathan Walker (Risk-Averse Expert)—Commentary

T bills are absolutely the safest investment to put your money into. There is no risk on the principal. Your interest will be paid by the U.S. government. This is the place to put money when you don't really know what you want to do with it, yet you want to make sure you have it when you want it. Money can be withdrawn from T bills at any time. The markets are extremely liquid.

F-64. DIAMONDS

Georgina Gold (Opportunistic Expert)—Commentary

Diamonds are tangible assets whose price fluctuates with their supply and demand around the world. You have made 25% on your money, which is a very good return on any type of investment. Over the long term diamonds represent a good investment since large, new supplies are not likely to be found and the DeBeers cartel, which controls most of the world's supply, has a vested interest in seeing the price go up over time. However, over the short term you could very easily see the price for diamonds drop sharply if there are changes in interest rates, political problems, and so forth. Therefore, you might want to cash in your gains at this point and look for a safer investment or be willing to withstand the risks and vagaries of the diamonds market.

F-1 For high return, take stock in yourself and Current Technologies. The stock appreciated 18%, or $48,336. Tough luck, the final value of your investment is $316,872, which is 36% below the average of the experts.

F-3 A man's worth is not his bond, especially 9% corporate bonds. The corporate bond yielded a very moderate 9%, or $22,356. Tough luck, the final value of your investment is $270,752, which is 45% below the average of the experts.

F-5 You'll never get rich, but also you'll never be poor. The CDs returned a straight 8.5%, or $21,107. Tough luck, the final value of your investment is $269,423, which is 45% below the average of the experts.

F-7 You don't need to save your pennies. The penny stock mutual fund picked the winners, and you earned a whopping 50%, or $113,907. Tough luck, the final value of your investment is $341,720, which is 31% below the average of the experts.

F-9 You can sleep well knowing your money is safe and sound. The corporate mutual fund returned 10%, or $26,334. Tough luck, the final value of your investment is $289,674, which is 41% below the average of the experts.

F-2   The safe are never sorry. The time deposits returned a predictable 9%, or $24,168. Tough luck, the final value of your investment is $292,704, which is 40% below the average of the experts.

F-4   The bulls turned out to be cows. Still, you made a more than respectable 12%, or $29,808. Tough luck, the final value of your investment is $278,204, which is 43% below the average of the experts.

F-6   Your future looks very cloudy indeed. The futures gained on 3%, or $7,449. Tough luck, the final value of your investment is $255,765, which is 48% below the average of the experts.

F-8   Backed by the full faith and obligation of the U.S. government, the T bills paid a moderate 8.2%, or $18,681. Tough luck, the final value of your investment is $246,494, which is 50% below the average of the experts.

F-10   You had a bad case of gold fever, which you're lucky did not kill you. The gold shares dropped, which means you lost 12%, or $31,601. Tough luck, the final value of your investment is $231,739, which is 53% below the average of the experts.

F-11 Hold on to your software, you're going for a ride. Spreadsheet $ystems was acquired by a company which paid a 25% premium, or $44,888, for your shares. Tough luck, the final value of your investment is $224,438, which is 54% below the average of the experts.

F-13 Security is investing in CDs and earning a decent return year after year after year. The CDs returned 9%, or $32,145. Tough luck, the final value of your investment is $389,315, which is 21% below the average of the experts.

F-15 Wallet heal thyself—the health of your wealth improved dramatically. The medical stocks did extremely well on the basis of new drugs and discoveries, yielding an impressive 100%, or $347,385. Congratulations, the final value of your investment is $694,770, which is 41% above the average of the experts.

F-17 No one complains about an 11.5% gain. The munis fund returned a pre-tax equivalent gain of 11.5%, or $19,282. Tough luck, the final value of your investment is $186,951, which is 62% below the average of the experts.

F-19 Bring home the bacon to celebrate. The pork bellies grew fat gaining 33%, or $42,370. Tough luck, the final value of your investment is $170,765, which is 65% below the average of the experts.

F-12   Average, average, average. The corporate bond income fund returned a predictable 9.5%, or $17,057. Tough luck, the final value of your investment is $196,607, which is 60% below the average of the experts.

F-14   There's no business as risky as show business. When the play closed opening night you were lucky (even with the CDs) to lose only 50% of your money, or $178,585. Tough luck, the final value of your investment is $178,585, which is 64% below the average of the experts.

F-16   Your investments are not taxing your wealth. The tax-free municipal fund yielded 11.2% (pre-tax equivalent), or $38,907. Tough luck, the final value of your investment is $386,292, which is 21% below the average of the experts.

F-18   Not bad for an absentee landlord. The real estate investment increased 20%, or $33,534. Tough luck, the final value of your investment is $201,203, which is 59% below the average of the experts.

F-20   Always safe and respectable. The corporate bonds yielded 10%, or $12,840. Tough luck, the final value of your investment is $141,235, which is 71% below the average of the experts.

F-21   It is more rewarding to avoid taxes rather than to pay them. The tax-free municipals you invested in returned a healthy pre-tax equivalent of 11%, or $13,397. Tough luck, the final value of your investment is $135,191, which is 73% below the average of the experts.

F-23   Write home to Mom and Dad for money. The penny stock fund struck out. Tough luck, the final value of your investment is zero. You are bankrupt.

F-25   Consistency can buy happiness, especially if it's paying 10% a year. The time deposits returned a profitable 10%, or $17,721. Tough luck, the final value of your investment is $194,935, which is 60% below the average of the experts.

F-27   Great products, like diamonds, are rare and valuable. Sales of Washout, Inc., despite company problems, continued to rise, as did the stock, which increased 50% in value for a gain of $241,656. Congratulations, the final value of your investment is $724,968, which is 47% above the average of the experts.

F-29   You rode the bull as the index continued to perform well. The Dow Jones Index increased 15%, or $29,038. Tough luck, the final value of your investment is $222,624, which is 55% below the average of the experts.

F-22   Not everyone gets rich on drugs. The medical drug fund was not a cure for your sick wallet, as it dropped in value 22%, or $26,795. Tough luck, the final value of your investment is $94,999, which is 81% below the average of the experts.

F-24   You'll never make the investment hall of fame. The T bills returned a modest 8.2%, or $2,291. Tough luck, the final value of your investment is $30,226, which is 94% below the average of the experts.

F-26   The 8% interest is less than interesting, but the bond showed you some appreciation. The total yield on the convertible bond was a solid 18%, or $31,899. Tough luck, the final value of your investment is $209,113, which is 57% below the average of the experts.

F-28   Certainly 9.5% of a half million dollars is okay. The corporate bond returned $45,915. Congratulations, the final value of your investment is $529,227, which is 8% above the average of the experts.

F-30   If all safe investments paid 11.2%, few people would ever gamble. The tax-free municipals yielded a good pre-tax equivalent rate of 11.2%, or $21,682. Tough luck, the final value of your investment is $215,268, which is 56% below the average of the experts.

F-31   It is a good feeling always to know where your money is. The CDs returned a predictable 10%, or $17,539. Tough luck, the final value of your investment is $192,924, which is 61% below the average of the experts.

F-33   Government mortgage investments are by, of, and for rich people. The Ginnie Maes yielded a healthy 12.5%, or $55,104. Congratulations, the final value of your investment is $495,935, which is 1% above the average of the experts.

F-35   Food commodities should be a staple on your investment plate. They and the CDs grew an appetizing 25%, or $19,593. Tough luck, the final value of your investment is $97,963, which is 80% below the average of the experts.

F-37   Return to the land. The real estate investment trust again gained a hefty 75%, or $460,845. Congratulations, the final value of your investment is $1,075,305, which is 119% above the average of the experts.

F-39   Sometimes diamonds are not precious stones. Diamonds, in the face of dumping by the Soviet Union, dropped 40% in value, or $154,493. Tough luck, the final value of your investment is $231,739, which is 53% below the average of the experts.

F-32   You ran the option play and scored. The options and T bills gained a combined 18%, or $31,569. Tough luck, the final value of your investment is $206,954, which is 58% below the average of the experts.

F-34   A convertible bond that warrants future investment. It was worth converting, so you made interest of 9%. Plus the bond appreciated 9%, for a total yield of 18%, or $79,350. Congratulations, the final value of your investment is $520,181, which is 6% above the average of the experts.

F-36   You can sleep like your money—safe and sound with little activity. The CDs returned an average 9.5%, or $7,445. Tough luck, the final value of your investment is $85,815, which is 83% below the average of the experts.

F-38   Not bad for the interim. The corporate bond showed a 10% increase, or $61,446. Congratulations, the final value of your investment is $675,906, which is 37% above the average of the experts.

F-40   If you can't think of anything else to do with your money. The asset management account paid 8%, or $30,899. Tough luck, the final value of your investment is $417,131, which is 15% below the average of the experts.

F-41   Take my T bills, please. The T bills paid a conservative 8.2%, or $25,830. Tough luck, the final value of your investment is $340,830, which is 31% below the average of the experts.

F-43   The rich shall inherit the earth—if they can avoid taxes. The tax-free munis yielded 11.2% (pre-tax equivalent), or $52,450. Congratulations, the final value of your investment is $520,750, which is 6% above the average of the experts.

F-45   Return to normalcy and to an 11.2% return. The fixed-rate municipals returned 11.2%, or $43,303. Tough luck, the final value of your investment is $429,939, which is 13% below the average of the experts.

F-47   Safety comes at a price. The government notes paid a lowly 9%, or $26,767. Tough luck, the final value of your investment is $324,180, which is 34% below the average of the experts.

F-49   Being an angel has finally paid off. The Broadway show on Martin Luther was a great success, attracting mass audiences and earning 200%, or $465,262, on your investment. Congratulations, the final value of your investment is $697,893, which is 42% above the average of the experts.

F-42   The stock never looked better—especially after losing money for three straight years. Spreadsheet Systems was acquired at a 25% premium, or $78,750. Tough luck, the final value of your investment is $393,750, which is 20% below the average of the experts.

F-44   Never look a gift horse in the circuits. The faltering Spreadsheet Systems was indeed taken over for a price 25% above the stock's current value, or $117,075. Congratulations, the final value of your investment is $585,375, which is 19% above the average of the experts.

F-46   The power bonds finally showed some energy. The power authority yielded a strong 14%, or $54,129. Tough luck, the final value of your investment is $440,765, which is 10% below the average of the experts.

F-48   Speculation is great—especially when it pays off. This Fortune 100 index fund gained a very respectable 18%, or $53,534. Tough luck, the final value of your investment is $350, 946, which is 29% below the average of the experts.

F-50   Bonds are to investing what ketchup is to food—essential but not too imaginative. The corporate bond yielded a straight 10%, or $23,263. Tough luck, the final value of your investment is $255,894, which is 48% below the average of the experts.

F-51   To the rich, "tax free" says it all. The 7% tax-free municipals returned the pre-tax equivalent of 11.2%, or $35,825. Tough luck, the final value of your investment is $355,693, which is 28% below the average of the experts.

F-53   This investment should have been optioned as the mining company came up empty-handed. The mining stock option dropped in value 22%, or $65,893. Tough luck, the final value of your investment is $233,619, which is 52% below the average of the experts.

F-55   Spreadsheet Systems finally racked up big points. The computer software company was acquired at a premium of 25% per share, for a gain of $50,593. Tough luck, the final value of your investment is $252,966, which is 49% below the average of the experts.

F-57   Faith and sound judgment paid off. The stock continued to rise, gaining 18%, or $39,244. Tough luck, the final value of your investment is $257,267, which is 48% below the average of the experts.

F-59   You have a good future as the Dow Jones Index continued its upward spiral. The futures paid a good 13%, or $21,442. Tough luck, the final value of your investment is $186,381, which is 62% below the average of the experts.

F-52 Power to the energy issues. The energy mutual fund grew a solid 15%, or $47,980. Tough luck, the final value of your investment is $367,848, which is 25% below the average of the experts.

F-54 Little ventured, little gained. The corporate bond yielded a moderate 10%, or $29,951. Tough luck, the final value of your investment is $329,463, which is 33% below the average of the experts.

F-56 It's the least you could do. The T bills earned a modest 8.2%, or $16,595. Tough luck, the final value of your investment is $218,968, which is 55% below the average of the experts.

F-58 Safety, like virtue, is its own reward. The corporate note returned the promised 9.5%, or $20,712. Tough luck, the final value of your investment is $238,735, which is 51% below the average of the experts.

F-60 There's nothing wrong with 10% a year. The time deposits yielded 10%, or $16,494. Tough luck, the final value of your investment is $181,433, which is 63% below the average of the experts.

F-61 Even neophytes sometimes win in the commodity game, as the demand for staples continued to exceed supply. The commodity index gained a strong 17%, or $22,879. Tough luck, the final value of your investment is $157,464, which is 68% below the average of the experts.

F-63 Back to basics. The T bills returned a fair 8.2%, or $12,541. Tough luck, the final value of your investment is $165,479, which is 66% below the average of the experts.

F-62   Banks are not where the money is. The CDs paid a moderate 9.5%, or $12,786. Tough luck, the final value of your investment is $147,371, which is 70% below the average of the experts.

F-64   The value of diamonds sunk when the Russians flooded the market. The diamonds you bought fell 40%, or $61,175. Tough luck, the final value of your investment is $91,763, which is 81% below the average of the experts.

MATCH WITS RATINGS

INVESTMENT	RATING
$600,000+	Extraordinary
$450,000–$599,999	Expert
$300,000–$449,999	Perceptive
$200,000–$299,999	Average
$100,000–$199,999	Fair
$0–$99,999	Poor

EXPERTS' FINAL INVESTMENT RESULTS

Chatsworth "Chat" Morton III	High Risk Strategy $585,375
Jonathan Walker	Risk Averse Strategy $194,935
Georgina Gold	Opportunistic Strategy $694,770

Average value of experts'
final investment total $491,693